Mona Siddiqui, OBE, is one of the UK's leading commentators on religious affairs. Professor of Islamic and Interreligious Studies at the University of Edinburgh, her publications include *How to Read the Qur'an*, *The Good Muslim* and *Christians, Muslims and Jesus*. She is a regular contributor to BBC Radio 4's 'Thought for the Day' on the *Today* programme and also to a wide range of programmes for BBC Scotland. She writes frequently for the national press and appeared on *Desert Island Discs* in 2012 in recognition of her contribution to public life.

'In his best novel, *The Power and the Glory*, Graham Greene observed that hatred was a failure of imagination. This is particularly true of religious hatred, which is an increasingly toxic element in the confusions that beset the human community today. Mona Siddiqui's new book is the perfect antidote to this virulent condition, because it invites us to enter imaginatively into the religious experience of a scholar from the Muslim tradition who expresses herself with rare wisdom and moderation. By sharing some of her most intimate experiences as a woman of faith who is also a grateful inheritor of the freedoms won by the Enlightenment, Siddiqui negotiates her way through the narrow defiles of religious disagreement with poise and grace. She has written a helpful and beautiful book.'

Richard Holloway, formerly Bishop of Edinburgh, author of *Looking in the Distance: The Human Search for Meaning* and of *Leaving Alexandria: A Memoir of Faith and Doubt*

'In this honest and moving account of a journey of faith, Mona Siddiqui addresses personal experiences of love and death, home and work, and belonging and otherness. Skilfully interweaving Islamic religious reflection about God and sex, human dignity and temporality, religion and multiculturalism, violence and forgiveness, the author has written a compelling narrative that displays throughout her conviction that "belief in God is about hope in life." All who search for meaning and for a life worth living, Muslims and non-Muslims alike, will learn and benefit from it.'

Miroslav Volf, Henry B Wright Professor of Theology, Yale University, author of *Allah: A Christian Response*

'Mona Siddiqui is one of our most important scholarly voices on Islam in the West. In this lovely book, we hear for the first time her own story. She writes from a deep place of authenticity and reflection about her own particular experiences, helping us to better understand the lives of millions of Western Muslims. It is that rare book, equally at home in the hands of a scholar, a student, or anyone wishing to learn more about what it means to be human.'

Amir Hussain, Professor of Theological Studies, Loyola Marymount University, and Editor of the *Journal of the American Academy of Religion*

'*My Way* couldn't be a more timely and eloquent reminder of how much value Islam places on education – for girls as well as boys. Mona Siddiqui's own personal journey is peppered with her considerable erudition on Muslim issues. This is a book everyone will gain from reading, whatever their background, and whether they be policymaker or interested general reader.'

Razia Iqbal, Presenter, BBC News

Best wishes Kara & hmm
M Siddiqui

MY WAY
A MUSLIM WOMAN'S JOURNEY

MONA SIDDIQUI

I.B. TAURIS
LONDON · NEW YORK

First published in 2015 by I.B.Tauris & Co Ltd
6 Salem Road, London W2 4BU
175 Fifth Avenue, New York NY 10010
www.ibtauris.com

Distributed in the United States and Canada Exclusively by Palgrave Macmillan
175 Fifth Avenue, New York NY 10010

ISBN: 978 1 78076 934 9
eISBN: 978 0 85773 510 2

A full CIP record for this book is available from the British Library
A full CIP record is available from the Library of Congress

Library of Congress Catalog Card Number: available

Printed and bound in Sweden by ScandBook AB

In memory of my parents

Contents

List of Plates

Acknowledgements

If you're lucky, you'll have someone encouraging you to write this kind of book. A book which doesn't quite fall into any particular genre but which says far more about the author than most of her other works. When I began writing I wasn't quite sure where I would end, but on completing the final chapter, I felt relieved and grateful to Alex Wright at I.B.Tauris who is the man behind this endeavour. He had spoken of this project several years ago and I had declined at first because I wasn't ready. But several years later, the project felt right. I want to thank Alex for his persistence and encouragement, and for his confidence in my ability to write a particularly personal book. Most of my academic colleagues to whom I have mentioned this work have also been supportive if a little curious, and many of my students have been intrigued; thank you all for your interest.

This book has been written against the backdrop of work and home life. It is the ordinary routine of our lives which inspires and challenges us to think about who we are and what gives meaning to our lives. My husband and my children have been part of this journey in many ways and it is their support and good cheer which I cherish whenever I sit down to write.

Note on Presentation

For ease of reading, I have avoided the use of diacritics in Arabic transliterations. I have also avoided italicising those Islamic terms or words which are now very familiar, such as Qur'an, hadith and shari'a. However, certain concepts have been presented with the Arabic equivalent in parentheses as I find that many readers wish to know what is the Islamic understanding of certain English words. Finally, Qur'an citations are based largely on Yusuf Ali's 1985 translation, *The Holy Qur'an*.

Foreword

'Dialogue between faiths' is generated at many different
levels. There is the seminar where texts are explored,
histories unravelled and interpreted, concepts clarified; there
is mutual witness, laying out why and how these doctrines
and practices matter in someone's identity; but there is also a
more vulnerable and more direct kind of witness which traces
the interaction of traditional commitments with a life in
contemporary society, reflecting on the challenges we share,
whatever our faith, in an intellectual and cultural world in
which faith is so often seen as a rather dangerous oddity.

This book is a moving and engaging example of this third
form of invitation to dialogue – or, better, to real conversation,
human exchange. Mona Siddiqui, undoubtedly one of the
best-known Muslim academics in the United Kingdom, uses
her exceptional skills as a communicator and her exceptional
experience of interfaith encounter to help us think about the
large issues of British culture and its ethics, global conflict
and spiritual integrity through the lens of her own candid
and penetrating meditations on a life lived in a variety of
contemporary contexts. A scholarly familiarity with all sorts
of questions in religious history and philosophy is combined
with sharp analytic discussion of current challenges. In these
pages we are never allowed to settle down with a lazy or

cliché-ridden account of the political and religious tensions of our world, but are consistently invited to think harder – and to listen harder.

It is a book written in the same vein as Mona Siddiqui's earlier and groundbreaking works on interfaith matters, but adds to their qualities a courageous willingness to locate all this against the backdrop of her personal development as both scholar and believer. Plenty of books are published that seek to advance understanding between faiths; not so many have this book's edge of personal exploration and honesty about the world we share in and through the diversity of our deep convictions. It is a very special and valuable addition to the literature of religious reflection in our time.

Rowan Williams
Master, Magdalene College, Cambridge

Preface

Benjamin Franklin wrote, 'Either write something worth reading or do something worth writing.' In this book I'm not sure I have done either, but the need to write something personal can occasionally become a kind of calling. I have written the book as a journey and it stands somewhere between autobiographical reflections and universal and contemporary themes of life. In the selection of material my aim has been to write about those events and questions which have touched my life but which are also of political, sociological and theological concern in the West.

As a British Muslim, I am writing from within the Islamic faith but not on behalf of other Muslims. My voice doesn't presume to represent or judge, but question. I do not see myself in the labels currently attached to people of religious faith such as conservative, modern, liberal, or secular. The only thing to say is that I was born into a Muslim family, raised a Muslim and have kept my faith with all the moral and ethical questions that any kind of religious belief should be open to in today's world.

Writing as an 'insider' requires the use of a certain vocabulary which I have tried to keep pertinent to the content of the book, but which is hopefully not too technical or obtrusive to a more general audience. Words such as God, Qur'an, prophet, divine love and eschatology will be familiar to theologians and scholars of religion and also to a general audience with some religious literacy. I speak of God here primarily as the ultimate sustainer and creator of the universe, the principal object of faith who is merciful and all knowing. I speak of the Qur'an and prophecy in the traditional Islamic understanding of a scriptural revelation, and Muhammad as a messenger of God. There is a long history of all kinds of intellectual and philosophical questions around these concepts which the faithful and the pious have posed to one another. So, while the book is primarily about material of a personal nature, focusing on themes of marriage, children, death and belonging, my aim is not just to tell stories of my life but to combine these stories with Islamic intellectual thought, past and present. Notable names such as Ghazali are frequently mentioned, and their words add theological depth. The book also mentions a variety of Western writers and literary figures whose works have influenced my thinking on so many of life's big questions. But this book is certainly not about any intellectual history of Islam; it is more a personal history with Islamic and other perspectives. My hope is that beyond the religious or academic audience, this journey will appeal to those who are quite simply interested in the questions of life.

The themes of this book have been a personal selection and perhaps the hardest section to write was the final chapter on God and how I think of God in my daily life. In many ways we as believers can take God for granted: he just is. Yet, belief isn't about certainty and providing answers. It's a constant search and struggle to find meaning in one's life and relationships. I have not mentioned any names in this book and hope that anyone who recognises themselves here will forgive me if I have been inaccurate or unjust in my portrayal. There are so many people and events who have not been mentioned, but writing is always about judgement. In the end I may not have said much but I hope I have said something.

ONE

Home: Past and Present

This book is not an autobiography but draws upon certain events and periods of my life to explore those personal, social and theological issues which shaped the way I grew up and which continue to challenge my thinking today. In some sense everything we write contains some glimmer, some reflection of our thinking and our personal lives. To understand a whole range of issues about faith, family and society, we have to delve into ourselves and be prepared for an introspective exploration. This journey may seem randomly pieced together as only certain events and themes have been selected, but the themes are those which have touched me as a person, as a Muslim and as a British citizen living at a time of extraordinary national and global change. Yet although all our lives are shaped by external factors, there is an internal spirit which challenges us all the time to think about ourselves in distinct and imaginative ways. There is no hiding or escape from the self, the way we let certain events and people settle inside as constant companions in life. It is this desire to look further into our own self which remains our biggest challenge in life. As Henry Thoreau wrote, 'What lies behind us and what lies ahead of us are tiny matters compared to what lives within us.'[1]

Yet, it is with how to make sense of what lies within us that I begin this reflective exercise. As you get older you spend more time thinking about the series of steps in life which brought you to where you are, about the exact moment when your existence started to take shape and made you who you are today and perhaps all that you can still become. As much as you try to think forward in your life, you still find yourself reflecting as much on the past as on the possibilities for the future.

I was born in Pakistan in Karachi and left that country when I was nearly five years old. I have hardly any memories of the Karachi I left behind in the 1960s, when my parents left to make the United Kingdom our home. But our journeys don't begin with our own hazy memories; they have a prior history and begin with the decisions taken by parents and grandparents of which we often have very little or no knowledge. We are always rooted in a more distant past and those of us who are lucky enough to have access to this past through stories passed down from generation to generation, by people who can tell us about another world, should consider ourselves fortunate. In exploring the theme of identities, the Arab Christian writer Amin Maalouf explains:

> In short, each of us has two heritages, a 'vertical' one that comes to us from our ancestors, our religious community and our popular traditions, and a 'horizontal' one transmitted to us by our contemporaries and by the age we live in. It seems to me that the latter is the more influential of the two, and that it becomes more so every day. Yet this fact is not reflected in our perception of ourselves, and the inheritance we invoke most frequently is the vertical one.[2]

It seems to me that in my case age has brought with it all kinds of questions, making me slightly restless. I'm not sure whether this is based on a sense that a part of me might belong elsewhere or the desire to just know more about my ancestors. I have no recollection of any conversation with any grandparent, and unfortunately our new life in England meant that I never would. A few years after we arrived in the UK, my only living grandparent died.

Our parents never discussed their move with us and in those early years we didn't see fit to ask them. They must have been similar to so many of their generation who just decided to leave the subcontinent in search of a different and hopefully better life in the UK. The first few years remain slightly hazy. But I now see that the main influences in our lives go back in history, to the early years of our parents' lives and all that which shaped and influenced them. It is in the stories which our parents tell us of their own childhood, their own dreams, that we understand why they took the decisions they did and how these decisions impacted on my own life. As I reflect on what my parents started with and what they became, it hits me just how much strength and courage my parents' generation had. They shared much of this past with people who became their friends, also from India or Pakistan, but no one ever discussed whether they had done the right thing in leaving their country of birth.

Whatever their reasoning and plans were, we were in the dark. But the vague sense of a return to Pakistan lingered in our home for several years. When it finally dawned on me that we were not going back, not even for regular visits, I remember feeling a profound sense of sadness. This was not because I remembered Karachi with any great fondness, but I was doubtful whether another country could ever become home. For years I would look up at an aeroplane and think that planes always took you away from places and that these long journeys were not about finding new horizons but about leaving behind those we love. Only in a rather old-fashioned album which we had brought with us from Pakistan there remained some black and white photos of another world. My favourite was the one with me, small but beautifully dressed as a bride for a school play, posing next to a childhood friend who had taken the role of the groom. For me it was not just a school play, but those two smiling faces represented the totality of the life I had left behind. I had come to the UK as a four-and-a-half-year-old and it wasn't until I was 13 that it dawned on me that there was no returning to another home; this was home forever.

Decades later I found myself slightly puzzled over an event which the Scottish National Portrait Gallery held for its reopening during 2011–12 under the title of *A Scottish Family Portrait* series. I was one of the families whose picture was taken, a British person of Pakistani heritage who had made a contribution to Scottish life. The commissioned photo of my family was excellent but I remember feeling a slight unease at the thought that I was in some ways linked to a migration story – I didn't see myself as a migrant; I was British and the UK the only home I had ever known.

I often wonder what my parents thought when they came to this country, in terms of our religious upbringing. How would they raise us in a home where religion mattered, the observance of faith mattered, yet in a very different context to the one they were used to? My family came from a Sunni Muslim background and we were raised as Muslims. The family context is often the place where one understands the presence of God and religion in one's life. It is primarily within the family that one embraces, nurtures or rejects religious faith. My parents did not spend time explaining the meaning of God to us; we just understood God in an Islamic context, as a merciful and transcendent being, close to us yet ultimately unknowable. Islam is not a religion with many rituals, but rituals punctuate the life of the believer in different ways, celebrations mark particular events within a religious faith, and individual or collective enactment of a ritual is a gift and a task. Family life is often intertwined with the rituals of faith so much so that a culture which is not connected to the transcendent may even seem hollow.

For the believer, participating in ritual activity is a re-enactment of a profound truth, that which makes one belong to a belief system drawing the believer nearer to God. Thus, religion was often externally expressed through ritual. The Qur'an itself refers to the believer and occasionally to the 'believing community' and mentions certain rituals which are a way of keeping God part of the daily rhythm of one's life: 'So read as much of the Qur'an as is easy for you. And establish prayers and give *zakat* and loan to Allah a beautiful loan' (Q73:20). Prayer, fasting, almsgiving, and even laws on food and drink, are a means to remembering God and provide a common language of worship between religions. But how each faith prays, fasts, observes the daily rituals says something about the faith and the believer's relationship with God. Islam has relatively fewer rituals than many religions, but God is remembered and invoked at all times in the life of the individual. The name Allah is mentioned so frequently in different phrases throughout the day that it is part of the daily vocabulary of many Muslims irrespective of their mother tongue. The simple *Bismillah* or 'in the name of God' are the words used before eating, drinking, beginning a journey, or simply uttered for no reason other than the mention of God. Although the Qur'an mentions different

forms of worship in various *suras*, it often groups together
two in particular: those who pray and give alms. There
are many instances of this, as in 'Perform prayers and give
alms' (Q2:110), or 'And they were not commanded except to
worship Allah, [being] sincere to Him in religion, inclining to
truth, and to establish prayer and to give zakah. And that is
the correct religion' (Q98:5).

It is important for parents to give their children some
sense of their heritage, to feel that they can live with various
identities and loyalties and not feel compromised. This is not
about holding onto some cultural ideal, a repetition of a past
age, but about creating a meaningful and connected context.
Our language, dress and food said something about us at
home and our religion provided the framework for how we
expressed all these differences. The meat we ate at home was
always meat which is coined as halal in popular usage, that is,
from a clinical and spiritual slaughtering of an animal prior
to consumption (*dhabiha*). I grew up knowing that dietary
prohibitions, however few in Islam, were about observance
and practice but in themselves didn't make someone virtuous.
So it is always interesting when people associate observance
with goodness. Many Muslims do consume meat which may
not be *dhabiha* with the justification of the Qur'anic verse,
'and the food of those who were given the Scripture is
lawful for you' (Q5:5), which includes Jewish and Christian
communities. This whole area becomes quite complex in
jurisprudence with different views within the Sunni schools
and also between the Sunnis and the Shi'a. But for me it
has been a relatively simple but meaningful observance, an
intrinsic part of the respectful pluralism of British society

Prayers and worship formed part of the culture which
my parents had nurtured. There were prayer mats in all the

bedrooms, as worship was quite a private act in our house. We didn't pray together as a family, but my mother would often gently remind us that it was time for prayer or that prayer time was passing. Eid at the end of Ramadan has probably been my favourite day, beginning with my father and brothers praying in the mosque and ending with a lavish gathering of family and friends at home. During the month of Ramadan, we fasted but I didn't always keep all the fasts. Worship was encouraged but never forced. Faith was about keeping God a constant presence in your life, however you observed its outward manifestation.

Eid at home was not without its tensions and disgruntlements. My mother's outlook was that the joy of Eid lay in the build-up to the day, not the actual day itself. It was the fasting and praying in the month of Ramadan, the last few days of frenzied activity to ensure everything was ready and the rigorous cleaning and tidying that were all part of Eid. Then there was the food, copious amounts of food cooked during Ramadan, *iftars* for so many friends and relatives and then the special cuisine reserved for Eid. But as a family, we never went anywhere for Eid. We always stayed at home and invited others, whether for breakfast, lunch or evening dinner. As children and even as young adults, we just helped out, never quite understanding why we always did the inviting, why we always had to cook so much and why my mother was so insistent that it was better to have guests than be a guest. She loved cooking and was an excellent cook and was partly trying to create the cultural environment she had experienced in her own childhood. But these were not the main reasons she insisted on this kind of hospitality and it wasn't until much later in my life that I understood the virtue of that kind of thinking. It was essentially based on the concept of giving, of generosity to others. Having people in your house, taking the time to cook for them, being a good host demands certain qualities. We have to be patient, diligent and bring out the best of what lies within us. This requires hard work, it requires the whole family to pull together, but most of all it requires that we think of others, that we share with others and that we make time for others.

This is not always easy. In our busy lives, with so many demands made on our time, taking time out for Eid can be an inconvenience for some. Determined by the lunar calendar, its precise day and date often leads to controversy within communities. When the morning prayers end and good wishes are exchanged, for many, Eid becomes just another day. This kind of thinking reduces faith to ritual alone, that somehow in obedience to God, we have done our duty. But Ramadan and Eid are not about observance of ritual alone. God does not gain anything by our obedience, for His majesty does not lack in anything. Rather, God tests us most in our relations to one another, for essentially the relationship between man and God rests on the relationship that human beings foster with one another.

In essence, Eid was about hospitality. Hospitality is a central virtue in most religious traditions. The most famous of the biblical references is probably Hebrews 13:2, 'Do not neglect to show hospitality to strangers for thereby some have entertained angels unawares.' In Islamic thought it is said that our hospitality towards one another generates a positive response from the angels themselves. Many traditions speak of angels not visiting the home of those who do not receive guests. The linking of hospitality with this kind of supernatural imagery makes well the theological point that being hospitable to others is essential to a good and virtuous character and synonymous with faith itself. Traditions abound in which the stranger and the guest are like blessings in our lives:

> The Emissary of God (may God bless him and grant him peace) was asked 'What is faith?' He said, 'The giving of food and the exchange of greetings.' 'In expiation and grades [of good deeds], he said, 'the giving of food and the praying by night while people are asleep [is best].' He was asked about the pilgrimage acceptable to God and he said, 'It is the giving of food and of goodly words.' Anas said, 'A house which is not entered by a guest is not entered by angels.'[3]

Islam, like all other scriptural traditions, has been enriched with stories and anecdotes about prophets and saints who shed light on how God works and tests humankind. A famous hospitality tradition is related to Abraham, one of God's chosen messengers but who was rebuked by God for refusing hospitality to a stranger:

> It is said that a Zoroastrian asked hospitality from Abraham, the friend [of God]; so he said: If you become a Muslim, I will give you hospitality. So the Zoroastrian passed on, and God revealed to him [Abraham]: you would not give him food except with his religion changed, and I have fed him for seventy years notwithstanding his unbelief. If you had given him hospitality for a night, what responsibility would have fallen on you? So Abraham set off running after the Zoroastrian and brought him back and gave him hospitality. So the Zoroastrian said to him: By what means did it become plain to you? So he mentioned it to him. And the Zoroastrian said to him: Does he deal with me in this way? Show me Islam so that I can become a Muslim.[4]

Hospitality is not confined to food alone, but food is so essential to hospitality that it is said we are accountable to God for all that we spend except the food we serve our guests; God himself would be embarrassed to ask about that.[5]

Yet although one's sense and attitude to religion often begins within the context of the family, it seems that scripture itself is directed more to the individual and their relationship with God rather than this family reality of many lives. We grew up with a sense that although rituals were intrinsic to faith, faith in God lay in something much deeper. Rituals provided a connection, they brought people together in a common purpose, in gratitude to God, in remembrance, but that God could neither be understood nor encapsulated in any religious ritual. God had to be felt as a presence inside you; once you had this relationship with God, you could never be alone.

Alongside this worship, the concepts of gratitude (*shukr*) and patience (*sabr*) were really where my parents' faith found meaning. My mother always reminded us how blessed life was even though religious faith brought with it its own trials. And without being particularly conscious of it, I gradually realised that whenever I spoke of God, I associated my belief in God with a way of looking at life as a whole rather than as a collection of rules to be obeyed. God was present in my relationships, my work, in a whole set of freedoms in the world. Belief was about seeing glimpses of the divine in the ordinariness of life, and in a way, that is fundamentally how I carried God inside me, within a perpetual conversation.

Being British and Muslim throughout school and university did not produce any real angst, for our cultural Islam was the Islam of a fairly conservative India/Pakistan which did not necessarily see the West as a polar opposite.

There was order in the Western way of life, civic society was harmonious and obedient to laws, there was no mob justice or the kind of insecurity and danger which could make going out of the house a problem, especially for women. There were no particular conversations about loyalty to faith as opposed to loyalty to the state, and I grew up feeling that I belonged to Britain despite occasional feelings of difference and even restriction in a country where everyone, especially young girls, had so many freedoms. There is only one conversation I remember having with my mother when I was in my late teens. She was trying to explain how and why she had raised us in her particular manner, where parental influence and educational influence on our lives was of the utmost importance. Her words encapsulated the dilemma that many people of her generation probably felt, but who I imagine lacked the wisdom and the confidence to enunciate either to themselves or to their children. She explained how she knew almost immediately on arrival in the UK that she would need to raise her family in a very different manner to the way she had been raised in India. She watched television, saw how people behaved with each other in the outside world and was unsettled – forced to rethink her views and attitudes. This was a country which did not just provide a new life but a new way of thinking about life. There was a freedom here which was both seductive and bold, but the challenges were to be embraced, not ignored and not feared.

What resources do parents use then when they experience a shift in consciousness about the most important thing they do – raising their children? That generation which arrived in the 1950s and 1960s was a relatively conservative generation who had left their homes in pursuit of money, education or both. They had left some of their traditions and customs behind, but most probably had very little understanding of how different the West was. Yet in many ways they showed a fearlessness, a courage and most of all an inner strength in making the decision to leave. And when it came to raising their children, they were alone, without the extended family, without the support of their own brothers and sisters. They were suddenly leading lives as individuals rather than as families and communities. I didn't appreciate the extent of this rupture in my parents' lives until much later on in my own adult life.

Whether it was school or home life, there were certain principles which defined who we were and who we were expected to become. At the heart of our upbringing was a sense that learning and seeking knowledge was indeed a religious duty and virtue and that it required cultivation. The Qur'anic prayer, 'O God increase me in my knowledge' (Q20:114), was often mentioned as a way that one could draw near to God through seeking knowledge, and that asking for more knowledge in all humility was a legitimate prayer. There was no distinction here between the religious and profane. My parents read all the time – not to preach to us, but for their own pleasure and possibly to inspire in us a love of literature, including religious literature; in many ways I don't think the distinction mattered to them. I think that therein lay a fundamental reason why a sense of belonging developed quickly in me. Allowing children intellectual freedoms may come with its own risks, but it can provide a rich interior, nurture a generation that doesn't just want to ask questions but also has a commitment to pursuing answers. This is not limited by where you live or grow up. We were free to think and explore, to read and question; there were no limits on discussion, and most importantly there were no unsuitable books. Maybe this is why I wanted to become a journalist when I was at university: to learn from other people's lives and stories, connecting the past to the present.

That emphasis on learning and seeking knowledge was not conveyed as a heavy burden in our home; rather, it was a kind of continuous conversation, often humorous, in which the lives of famous saints, scholars and theologians were casually dropped in. The lives of those who were near to God, through their worship, learning and devotion, served as important figures and worth recounting, and for much of my life at home, my mother mentioned names whose real significance I was only to grasp much later in my own academic training. When my mother talked to us about the intellectual giants of the Islamic world, I was often left confused over the chronology of people and events. Who came first, what happened when and the whole Arab/Persian background to so much of our Indian Islamic heritage was so intriguing yet remained very disjointed in my head.

But it has gradually dawned on me that knowledge is a divine gift, not confined to the religious sphere of any one religion, and that the pursuit of knowledge in every great faith is inextricably linked with the great virtues of justice, hope and love. The Arabic word 'ilm is most often used to render knowledge, but as Franz Rosenthal says, the word knowledge 'falls short of expressing all the factual and emotional contents of 'ilm'. Rosenthal is right to assert that ''ilm is one of those concepts that have dominated Islam and given Muslim civilisation its distinctive shape and complexion.' He argues that the word has been operative as the major determinant of Muslim civilisation through its all-pervasive depth and use, even more so than a word as powerful as *tawhid*, the recognition of the oneness of God. Rosenthal writes:

> There is no branch of Muslim intellectual life, of Muslim religious and political life and of the daily life of the average Muslim that remained untouched by the all pervasive attitude towards 'knowledge' as something of supreme value to Muslim being. *'Ilm* is Islam even if the theologians have been hesitant to accept the technical correctness of this equation. The very fact of their passionate discussion of the concepts attests to its fundamental importance for Islam.[6]

In the Islamic tradition, the pursuit of knowledge is a duty and a gift. But there is also a strong sense that knowledge is perfected only when it is followed by doing what is right, doing what is good. Religious faith itself can be emptied of dogma and doctrine, but it will always hold good deeds as noble values in themselves; good deeds are what God himself desires. As the Qur'an says, 'If God had wanted, He could have made you one community. So compete with one another in doing good deeds, so that He may test you by what he has given you' (Q5:48). Then there is the famous hadith which encapsulates charitable behaviour in its widest sense, 'Each person's every joint must perform a charity every day the sun comes up: to act justly between two people is a charity; to help a man with his mount, lifting him onto it, hoisting his belongings onto it is a charity, a good word is a charity, every step you take to prayers is a charity and removing a harmful thing from the road is a charity.'[7] Good deeds are themselves acts of worship reflected through the principle of humankind's accountability to one another. We look for God in worship and in prayer, but we fail to see God where He is most present. One of the most important traditions is that God will say on the Day of Resurrection:

> O son of Adam, I fell ill and you visited Me not. He will say: O Lord, and how should I visit You when You are the Lord of the worlds? He will say: Did you not know that My servant So-and-so had fallen ill and you visited him not? Did you not know that had you visited him you would have found Me with him? O son of Adam, I asked you for food and you fed Me not. He will say: O Lord, and how should I feed You when You are the Lord of the worlds? He will say: Did you not know that My servant So-and-so asked you for food and you fed him not? Did you not know that had you fed him you would surely have found that (the reward for doing so) with Me? O son of Adam, I asked you to give Me to drink and you gave Me not to drink. He will say: O Lord, how should I give You to drink when You are the Lord of the worlds? He will say: My servant So-and-so asked you to give him to drink and you gave him not to drink. Had you given him to drink you would have surely found that with Me.[8]

Thus, the true search for God does not lie in books of philosophy or theology but in the hospitality of human relationships.

My parents were proud but not sentimental in character. At times they would become nostalgic about India and mention the British Raj. These conversations did not turn into tedious history lessons as such, but little snippets of the way they thought about their own past. They were of a generation for whom stories of the Empire and memories of partition were part of their lives. Their occasional reflections were frustrated mutterings about what the British took from India, notably the Kohinoor diamond, as well as more sombre acknowledgements of what the British had contributed, like the rule of law, improved transportation, the English language and a unified postal system. My father would explain why India was the new jewel in the crown after the British had lost the American colonies. However, he always tried to impress that in the midst of exploitation and degradation, much of the British legacy had been constructive. But when I went to India for the first time, none of that mattered to me; I just wanted to meet my relatives, people whose names had been dropped in so many conversations, and get an understanding of my parents' past lives.

My first trip to India took place when I was in my mid-20s. My sister was getting married and it was to be a big event. It was my first trip to Delhi and then Bihar. Everything about this trip promised excitement: the wedding, meeting my aunts, uncles and cousins, and my very own personal treat – ten days of touring on my own around Delhi and Agra. My parents had both left half their families in India when they moved to Pakistan after partition in 1947. It wasn't something which troubled them, but they often talked of growing up in India as well as of their life in Pakistan. So when the opportunity arose, I wanted to see where my father had come from, the small village which remained home to his brothers and sisters but which he left behind forever when he went to medical school in the city.

The wedding was an experience of family politics: warm, cruel and inviting all at the same time. We hadn't grown up in an extended system, so the emotional and physical challenges of how families and couples lived in close proximity, often in the same house, was intriguing. However, I found the intensity and the lack of privacy unappealing. Everyone knew everything and what they didn't know they just assumed or made up. It is strange how people can make you feel, even if they don't express it openly. We were the family who had

left, made a new life in a faraway land and were returning for
the first time. We spoke English and thus, it was assumed,
imagined ourselves to be different, and that meant superior.
We were different in so many ways, but our fluency in Urdu,
our relaxed manner of simply being Indian Muslims while we
were there, made them feel at ease – we weren't superior, we
just lived in England.

After the wedding I knew I wanted to go to see the village
where my father had grown up. It would be a long, and indeed
tortuous, journey, but it was almost like a moral imperative.
I went accompanied by a male cousin, not knowing what to
expect and how I would be received. It was night time when
we eventually arrived, hot, tired and quite disoriented. A
couple of lanterns lit the entrance to the house and I heard
someone shout out, 'Ali's daughter has arrived, look' (Ali
was my father's name). But even though I was exhausted, I
could barely hide my shock. Everyone greeted me with such
warmth, but all I could think of was how did these people
live like this? No running water, no real electricity, hardly
any household furniture. I had always been told that at one
time the family had been quite affluent in terms of land and
property, but where was it now? Had it just been squandered
or had they just made bad and lazy decisions? It was so hot,
but there was no way of cooling yourself, and after spending
one night there, I thanked them, said my goodbyes, and left.
It sounds unkind, but I was so grateful that my father had
had the courage and the vision to leave for the sake of his
education and make something of his life. I couldn't quite
picture him growing up with so little but he had, though for
him life changed. Once my mother had told me that it was
an aunt who had showered my father with much love and
encouraged him towards a career in medicine, recognising his

potential. Sometimes the love and encouragement of just one person is all you need to imagine a different kind of life for yourself. His aunt must have known that he would never be able to fulfil his potential had he stayed there. Yet my father never said an unkind word about that village.

I always knew my father was very bright but it has only recently dawned on me the extent of his passion for learning. Medicine was his profession and he had become a consultant psychiatrist and worked all his life until he suffered a stroke. But he was interested in religious literature, poetry, all kinds of imaginative writings which he could read in Urdu, Persian, English and probably Hindi as well. I heard Rumi and Attar from him as well as Ghalib and Iqbal. He had smiled approvingly when he saw my first attempt at reading *Pride and Prejudice*. He told me it was a classic of world literature. When I went to that humble village which he had left, I wondered how he had achieved his own learning, how his own passion for education had developed when it had clearly not been a family trait. I could see no intellectual only physical resemblances between my father and his siblings. I often thought he must have been quite lonely being so different from the others.

Perhaps being different made it easier for my parents to leave their families. But my parents weren't just wise, they were also young at heart. When I visited Pakistan and met with my mother's family, I again recognised that she too was different in her thinking from the rest of her family. They were an extremely good looking family, especially my uncles whose handsome looks never waned, but my mother seemed to be an independent spirit, a woman who wanted to break away, and marriage to my father made that possible. She told us that as a young girl she had wanted a formal education and was thinking of nursing as a career yet she was married very young and marriage changed everything. My parents lived in various places, including Saudi Arabia, but wherever they lived, my mother stayed at home to look after the home and family and my father went to work. They didn't expect to live their lives outside this norm and neither did we.

It is true that we never really discussed why they came to the UK, but I always assumed that education, economics and opportunities were too compelling. My father wanted to gain further qualifications and over the years both my parents must have thought that West Yorkshire, where I grew up, was a good and safe place to raise a family. We saw how hard my father worked, often in distant places, but he never complained and I often wondered whether my parents had any regrets. Even if they did, they found solace in their shared passion for reading and this brought them closer. I often sensed that though my mother was far more enterprising than my father, they shared a few personality traits, both holding a quiet but mutual respect for each other's intellect. This was what made their marriage a marriage of equals. Throughout their lives, the love of literature created a special bond between them. My parents didn't differentiate fiction from religious literature. For them, learning didn't have boundaries; they didn't create false distinctions between wisdom literature and popular short stories. This was reflected in their attitude to our education and where I first understood a real difference between me and my school friends. This emphasis on higher forms of education meant that a university education was a given. I would often joke with my school friends that in middle-class Asian families, it was inconceivable that a child would not go to university: it was a sign of failure. I must have sounded like such a geek, but I thought higher education was what everyone aspired to.

When I was applying for university along with my friends, my peers, mainly white and British, had a choice in what they wanted to do with their lives, whereas my family friends, mainly Asian, Muslim and largely middle class, faced limited choices. The top tier was to become a doctor or possibly a dentist; the second was law and, at a squeeze, accountancy; other choices were unfortunately often dismissed. Failure for many of my parents' friends was not so much not getting into university, but rather not getting into medicine. Even though my father would have loved for us all to be doctors, this was never an issue in the family and we were allowed to pursue different careers. For her daughters, my mother had already picked out career paths: doctor, barrister and lecturer – and we did exactly that.

A generation later, as I write this book, my middle son is going to university to study medicine. I miss not being able to tell my parents this news, and seeing their pride in knowing that their hopes live on in their grandchildren. Yet I wonder how much has changed and whether access to higher education has remained a class issue far more than it has an ethnicity or gender issue. In January 2013, the Universities Minister, David Willets, said that universities in England should be doing more to encourage applications from the white working class, as boys generally seem to be underperforming in higher education. University education, in terms of courses, access and cost, has become a bit of a minefield and it seems to me that irrespective of whether government targets and quotas really change attitudes, we may be missing a more basic point which is how do we get families of all backgrounds to value education and foster the culture of learning? University education provides different things for different people, but the desire for knowledge and the respect for learning of all kinds go well beyond a degree and must come at a much earlier stage in our lives. Only then does its presence continue to enrich our mind and soul throughout our whole life.

Maybe this is why, when I look at some Muslim families today, I see a different kind of tension – the clash between religious knowledge and secular professions, the idea that spiritual growth comes from living apart from this world or that it is only religious knowledge which can strengthen your faith in God. I believe this has produced a cultural malaise in which basic books of theology suffice as learning and the dissemination of empirical and scientific knowledge, of literature, music and the arts, is seen by some as weakening the faith. I personally can't see this when I look at the rich history of Islamic civilisation or even the way the Qur'an commands us all to reflect upon the world, encouraging bold and free inquiry, not a closed and trapped piety. In Islamic history, the period between the ninth and eleventh centuries saw some of the best of human free thinking. The combination of a religious faith and an almost obsessive thirst for knowledge is found in the reign of the controversial ninth-century Abbasid Muslim ruler, al-Mam'un, during whose rule we find a golden age of Arabic science. The scientists, writers and philosophers al-Mam'un brought together were not all Muslim, but it was precisely this cross-fertilisation of ideas, discoveries and sheer experimentation by people from all backgrounds that created this unrivalled period in Islamic civilisation. The scientific revolution of this age paved the way for many later European discoveries, but it also sat comfortably with the emergence of deep theological and mystical writing. There were no crude opposites in this world between science and religion because both in their own ways gave hope.

Today much of the Islamic world continues to have sophisticated conversations about bioethical issues, but at a time when the overall religious rhetoric of Islam has become more insular, it is important to project this past intellectual spirit into the present world. For me, the simplest and most potent Qur'anic prayer is 'O Lord increase me in knowledge' (Q20:114). Seeking knowledge in all its diversity with all its risks is central to seeking God and understanding ourselves. This is what we need to encourage in young people, as much as reinforcing the utilitarian aspect of higher education. A good education may lead to a good profession, but if we can foster a desire for knowledge alongside it, this can transform your very person.

Furthermore, we spoke with our parents in Urdu and were raised bilingual. Their wisdom in ensuring we learnt Urdu meant that we could always talk to them but also we could always remain connected to two different cultural contexts. I think that to truly understand the essence and nuances of any culture, it's vital to know the language, to at least be able to speak the language. The other means by which Urdu continued to influence our thinking was through music. I listened to songs and *ghazals* – poetry sung to music – written by some of the best poets and felt drawn to another world where the lyrics and manners of love were so different and beautiful. Yet what they all shared was the pain of love and the human desire to own the unattainable. Knowing a language isn't just about knowing words and getting by. If language is a connection with the present, it is also a connection with a heritage. Today, I find myself relentlessly encouraging my children to speak in Urdu at home. English is their main language, probably their mother tongue, but Urdu opens up another culture for them without reducing their feelings of being British.

It is true that our lives were divided into public and private but for the most part not our principles. We may have dressed differently, observed dietary restrictions and never been completely at one with the various kinds of 'white' British cultures in which we grew up, but for me personally my sense of identity was never about 'us and them', more 'us with them'. This is not to misrepresent the huge social and political changes taking place in Britain in the 1970s and 1980s. At school, one could at times be subjected to mild racism and I am sure that we were often unaware of the various subtleties of prejudice around us. But looking back, neither the colour of our skin nor our faith limited us; we were brought up to believe that aspiration and ambition weren't ugly words, but rather that it was only through aspiration that you could change society.

Whether we define it as institutional or individual, racism today makes us feel uncomfortable because somehow it sounds like a dated prejudice. We should all have moved on by now. The only problem is that racism is only one form of prejudice and that prejudice in all its guises lives within us all, whatever our background or the colour of our skin. Growing up in this country, I felt hurt by the odd incident of playground racism, but I humoured the lingering prejudices which my own parents and their friends had brought over to the UK from the subcontinent. They would sometimes make jokey remarks about other ethnic groups from India or Pakistan, their language or mannerisms; this kind of intra-cultural humour, while never malicious, could easily verge on mild condescension. Maybe because we all came largely from a similar and shared background it didn't seem like prejudice, but it was and it has stayed with me, still making me uncomfortable about my own prejudices. There is a kind of tribalism in us all which makes us feel uncomfortable, even threatened at times by difference. But our prejudices often tell us more about ourselves than we would like to admit. When the Qur'an says 'we have made you into nations and tribes so you may get to know one another', the verse reads like a divine blessing in our lives, but getting to know one another demands hard work, patience and most of all a generous heart. It seems to me that with the breakdown of family living, the forces of globalisation and large scale migration have created a different kind of struggle – fractured societies where people are struggling to find ways of recreating familiarity, a sense of belonging to something and a sense of community.

In recent times, however, the Islamic faith has been viewed with varying degrees of suspicion, forcing an atmosphere of political correctness. In 2008, the writer and comedian Ben Elton made the remark that 'the BBC will let vicar gags pass but they won't let imam gags pass'. He was making the point that political correctness had made some authorities scared to make jokes about Muslims or Islam for fear of upsetting radical elements in the faith. The question that was being posed was essentially 'Why can't Muslims take a joke?' In a world where everything is up for critique, where nothing remains sacred anymore, why should religion – and for that matter, only one religion – be exempt from global commentary? Today freedom of expression is lauded as the ultimate triumph of robust liberal democracies. Religious faith forms one aspect of society and remains open to both protection and objection. I was alarmed that so many people carried this perception of Islam, because for me, religion is only strengthened by humour. The ability to see the good with the bad, the gifts and the problems of faith, demands that we be honest and reflective and willing to engage with a wide array of cultural and social perspectives. The ability to see ourselves as others might see us is a sign of humility; the ability to laugh at ourselves is a sign of confidence and maturity. Self-criticism is not a weakness and reminds us that we take neither ourselves nor what we believe to be the only moral arbiters of any society.

In one generation so much has changed in terms of attitudes to race, gender and sexuality. A sense of confidence and conviction in who you are is a good thing, but we must always remain open to the elements of surprise and shock in our lives, those events which jolt us out of our complacency and encourage us to rethink the faith, the identities and values we thought defined us. A couple of years ago I was speaking to a well-known German theologian who told me that his daughter, a church-going Protestant, was marrying a Hindu man and that although he had found the concept of a mixed faith marriage difficult at the beginning, he had accepted it for his daughter's happiness. I found his honesty moving but also slightly troubling. I thought if faced with a similar situation as a Muslim, how would I react? Perhaps not as generously as him – and then I started wondering why not.

Throughout all the experiences of growing up, we knew Britain was our home and home means you develop a sense of belonging despite differences. We have become a society obsessed with issues around identity and labelling. My identity was encapsulated in the words British Muslim, but as a family we were always physically and mentally outside the wider Muslim communities around us. I think it was partly because our parents were quite reserved in their own way and this meant we never seemed to fit in completely anywhere. That feeling of being a slight misfit can be a problem, but it makes you think how much of your early life shapes your attitude to life forever. We were different from our Muslim family friends as well, those who gave their daughters far more social freedoms while we seemed to spend so much of our time at home.

When did I feel these differences the most? It was not when I was engaged in something specific to my culture or religion; it was when I couldn't be fully immersed in British culture. I think I felt this the most at Christmas. Whatever one says about Christmas having lost its true meaning, becoming too commercialised or celebrated only as a cultural phenomenon, it is an inviting all-consuming time. It isn't just that Christmas looks beautiful, the way it is packaged, advertised and sold, but the sense that no other religious festival can quite match up to it. It would be no exaggeration to say that no other religious or cultural occasion features as much in the global consciousness. Yes, people of different religious faiths in different parts of the world can be passionate about their own celebrations, but here in the West, everyone simply assumes that everyone else is part of this season. In fact many are genuinely surprised if you tell them you don't celebrate Christmas and even feel a little sad for you; you can see it in their faces. At school, when friends asked what celebrating Eid meant, the tentative reply was often, 'It's the Muslim Christmas' – but without tinsel, tree and turkey, it all rang a bit hollow. You had to explain that you didn't celebrate Christmas and they looked at you in sympathy at all the presents you were denying yourself. This question has a way of reinventing itself in each generation. My youngest son asked me once why we didn't have a Christmas tree. When I told him that we didn't celebrate Christmas, he replied, 'It's boring being a Muslim.' I tried not to laugh too much at this theological challenge because it occurred to me that he might have a point. How do you keep your religion engaging and meaningful when it can often appear as a contrast to so much that is familiar around you?

Christmas has always been a holiday for everyone living here, so invariably it is spent with family. But for a long time Christmas made me sentimental for what I hadn't experienced. I had rarely celebrated any Muslim festival in a dominantly Islamic society, where these festivals become a focal point of the calendar and the whole country is then bound by the same holiday spirit. This may be simple sentiment on my part in the whole story of what it is to belong. But the feeling remained with me for a long time and even now a small part of me can feel like this when I admire beautiful Christmas trees, glistening lights and holly and ivy garlands on the neighbourhood doors. Britain is my home; its cultures, language and opportunities continue to shape me as a person. I have never felt any real conflict living my Islam here and maybe this slight yearning is essentially about living with something which you cannot embrace wholeheartedly. I have happily exchanged cards and gifts with friends as a child and as an adult throughout this period, but always as an outsider. Perhaps there is no answer to this and the only expectation I should have of myself is to try to be as generous in someone else's celebration as I hope they are in mine. Giving and receiving is symbolic of divine generosity and always worthy. At times, the only way to view another's ritual is through respectful even joyous observation. Today, I can see that it is easier to just go along with people's assumptions rather than engage in the look of surprise even disappointment on their faces. So when shopkeepers ask in a jovial spirit at this time, 'Are you ready for Christmas?' I just reply, yes; it's the kindest thing to do.

My parents' migration to England denied me to some extent the great heritage of the subcontinent. They left their home so that we could make the UK our home. Having multiple belonging is enriching but can leave you feeling rootless. But over the years, I have learnt that the past is simply a series of moments that brings us to where we are today, that home is not some romantic ideal. Home is not just where we have come from, but is also where we are going. Home is what we make of the here and now; home is people, not a place; what we give to and receive from the community where we live and work; our relationships with those who are part of our daily lives.

My father may have known very little of the life he was to experience in the UK when he first came. But my parents remained enthusiastic and hopeful all their lives about us because they had been able to give us an education; it was enough to inspire us to do something worthwhile. Today I find myself constantly telling my own children that a good education stays with you forever as an eternal gift. But perhaps the greatest thing about education is that it sets you free, allowing you to become all that you can, however you start off in life. As I look at my own children today, my eldest son at university, and the middle one preparing to go, I understand how a sense of belonging is so essential to any idea of home. But young people need different kinds of reassurances. They live at a time when the world can appear on a screen in front of them at the simple click of a mouse, and while they may feel empowered through this connection, this is no substitute for the normal experiences which will shape their identities. A good education is not enough to ensure that your child remains focused and inspired. My son tells me quite openly that he is motivated by money, but that his career must mean something, it has to be intellectually and emotionally challenging and not just financially rewarding. Life has to be meaningful in all kinds of ways, and as parents we don't want our children to struggle – but maybe we are making a mistake. A little struggle is good; it keeps children appreciative of the things that matter.

The biggest distinction I see between the way I was raised and the way in which I am raising my children is to do with happiness. My parents' generation didn't really mention happiness much; for them, what seemed to matter more was worthiness. I don't know whether our happiness was just assumed or whether a generation ago people in general didn't talk about it much. Yet as the Persian poet Hafiz says, 'When all your desires are distilled you will cast just two votes, to love more and be happy.' We all want to be happy and it is this desire that makes all our lives different and yet the same. How did I envisage happiness as a young woman? I think I wanted freedom to be what I wanted to be; I didn't associate it with any one person until much later in life. But when my parents became ill, I experienced a different kind of happiness which lay in ensuring that I could be there for them in whatever way possible. It was a sense of duty mixed with doing for someone else. It sounds naive and it may never have been fulfilling, but at the time this kind of happiness was still real and tangible. Doing for them, being there for my mother when my father became ill, made me realise that no kind of happiness is fixed in life but that whatever time you spend doing for others is a blessing which returns to you as a blessing throughout your whole life.

I realise that I have begun to wonder why more people don't talk of happiness, as if it is too elusive, and that a noble life concerns itself with other matters. But happiness matters even though we are so often led to believe that happiness is beyond our reach, an imagined state and that the nearest we can come to happiness is a feeling of contentment. It may well be that most of our lives are about contented living, with unadulterated moments of happiness, but that does not make the happiness any less real. Happiness is a state of mind, of feeling that we are doing our best, that we are part of meaningful relationships. Happiness doesn't mean that we can avoid suffering or discomfort, but it requires that we surface as more thoughtful and mindful human beings throughout the problems of life, to be survivors.

We love our children but we can also guide our children to be loving towards others, to be happier because there is a clear connection between the two. Children don't always just grow out of certain kinds of behaviours, whether it is mood swings, bad manners or morose outlooks on life – they have to be nurtured and disciplined into thinking in another way. Overall I can honestly say that I have been blessed with happy children, but once, when my middle son seemed to be going through a less than happy time with some of the people in his school, I remember asking him why he was with this particular group, around whom he was clearly not flourishing emotionally. I told him, 'Don't spend your life with people who bring out the worst in you – life is too short – so spend it with people who have a good and positive effect on your life and can help you grow.' I realised then how important friendships are for everyone, but especially for younger people: friendships are the defining relationship of the modern age and young people reflect so much of their thinking and values around their friends. In recent years, many of the most poignant conversations I have had with my children have been about their relationships with their friends. And this is important because friendship isn't just a private matter, something we do in our own time and space. Because we need friends in our search for emotional and intellectual wellbeing, friendship is a bit like love, and can be transformative in its effects. Cultivating meaningful friendships has an immensely powerful social worth and I think is essential for the good of society, for human flourishing. The classical philosophers knew this. They regarded friendship as the most important ingredient of a worthwhile and happy life, essential to creating a good society, and argued that we can't be moral citizens without people around us. Aristotle famously said that 'no one would choose to live without friends, even if he had all the other good things'.

Friendship has a social and a personal worth, and while technology such as Facebook allows people to reconnect with the past, I find it curious as to why as we get older we start living more in the past and wondering what happened to the friendships we lost or never maintained. I must confess I moved away from my home town, from my university town, and struggled to keep contact with many who came into my life. But life makes you unexpectedly think about all kinds of relationships. For example, when my family first came to the UK, we lived in Cambridge and I began school there at the age of four and half. I have no memories of that school or the teachers or any of the pupils. I have only one memory, which is that of walking around the playground with a little boy who always had a big smile; he would hold my hand and talk to me in English. I didn't speak a word of English then and replied in Urdu – neither of us understood each other's language, but we understood each other. I don't remember his name or anything else about him, but he was probably my first friend in this country and today he pops into my head regularly – I think of him and curiously enough find myself missing the friendship I never got to nurture. The past we thought we'd left behind never really leaves us.

TWO

Marriage and Desire

In his acclaimed work, *Letters to a Young Poet*, Rainer Maria Rilke wrote that 'Love is hard. Love between one person and another; that is perhaps the hardest thing it is laid on us to do, the utmost, the ultimate trial and test and proof, the work for which all other work is just preparation.'[1] I think that Rilke is right in that love between two people, loving others, remains both our biggest joy but also our biggest challenge in life. We yearn to be loved and yet so often we find it difficult to love or to explain love. Robert Frost wrote that 'Love is an irresistible desire to be irresistibly desired.' But Rumi's observation that 'When the pen was busy writing, it was fluent, when it reached the word Love, it broke down' is one of the most powerful and haunting lines about our human struggle to define love. Yet when we love we also act. Love in all its manifestations, between partners, lovers, children and parents, siblings or between friends, demands that we devote a large part of our lives to thinking of others but also doing for others. Most of us carry a moral impulse and desire to do this as it is essential to our sense of humanity and wellbeing. The need to love and be loved is the most fundamental human need and it is this need which many rightly claim makes life worthwhile.

At times, people can describe our thinking and doing for others in terms of sacrifice or compromise, but these words carry a negative, restrictive sentiment implying that so many of our relationships prevent us from living our own lives freely, being who we really are. But it is precisely the opposite which is true, for we are not simply individuals acting on our own in this world. We deceive ourselves if we think of our existence as apart from others rather than among others. Human life and development occurs within a network of relationships; these relationships can influence our personal choices in various ways, but it is only by living with and within our relationships that our lives become meaningful. The relational aspect of our lives, the bonds of love which connect us to one another, lie at the core of our fundamental human experiences. We can neither be good nor bad, moral nor virtuous, outside of our relationships. Even if we regard our solitude as precious or hold a poetic lament that we are in the end only solitary beings, so much of the wisdom around us tells us that it is only when we know how to give of ourselves that we experience the true meaning of life. As Mitch Albom writes in *Tuesday with Morrie*, too many people live with meaningless lives because they're chasing the wrong things. The dying Professor Morrie's advice is 'Devote yourself to loving others, devote yourself to your community around you, and devote yourself to creating something that gives you purpose and meaning.'[2]

Our own religious faith is often tested through our relationships because it is these relationships which give depth to our lives. This seems to be the basic premise of how religious faith structures the ideal society: that is, one where people are always aware of their obligations to one another within the larger understanding of their obligation to God. When the Qur'an refers to human emotions, for the most part it doesn't do so in any abstract, philosophical or romantic sense, but in the framework of ties, whether they are marital, familial or commercial. The Qur'an doesn't talk of human singularity or solitude, even in worship, but for the most part conveys its message to people in relational settings. The variety of human relations mentioned in the Qur'an contain a moral dimension: in life, relationships are serious matters. Relationships involve a continuous weighing up of rights and responsibilities and demand that we observe our commitments as part of a righteous and well-lived life. Here, the language of passion and romance is absent, but the language of mutuality and compassion is present.

It seems to me that the two most important relationships which emerge are those between the believer/believing community and God, and between men and women. The overarching narratives of justice (*'adl*) and mercy (*rahma*), the two defining attributes of God, also shape our moral thinking towards one another in society. In so doing, the various themes in the Qur'an appear far less concerned about defining men and women in terms of gender attributes or binary oppositions. The Qur'an is concerned with the moral dimensions of people's relationships, and here, gender and sexuality are pivotal to the dialectic between God, man and woman. The masculine and the feminine are connected in all kinds of ways, and sex and sexuality are essential to this connection. As the Qur'an says, 'O Mankind, keep your duty to your Lord who created you from a single soul and from it created its mate and spread from these many men and women' (Q4:1). It is the primal couple who form the prelude to all creation, but it is only when they become destined for the earth that the social and moral relationship between men and women emerges.

What inspires all human activity and relationships is desire. In the famous words of William Irvine, it is desire which animates life: 'Banish desire from the world and you get a world of frozen beings who have no reason to live and no reason to die.'[3] Desire is an essentially personal aspect of human life. According to the Iranian philosopher Mutarda Mutahhari, the touchstone of man's humanity, is 'the presence of insights and beliefs'.[4] This, he argues, is the source of human civilisation and culture. Both humans and animals perceive themselves and their external world, striving to achieve their desires and objects in the light of their awareness and cognition. However, human desire differs in its 'scope, extent, breadth of awareness, cognitions and in the levels to which his desires and objects rise'.[5] It is in this ability to desire beyond our immediate locality of space and time that Mutahhari views as the wellspring of human civilisation. While such desire creates and animates humanity, it also necessitates regulation for the good of others, for the good of human relations. It is how we respond to our desires that makes them good, or indeed bad, not the desire itself.

Perhaps the most elaborate theological and philosophical treatment of human desire relates to sexual desire. For society to flourish we need to understand the sexual impulse and human desire in all its beauty but also in its excesses. Quite simply, Islam views human sexuality and desire, erotic love, as intrinsic to the fullness of human experience. Sexual desire compels us to reflect upon life and upon our deepest vulnerabilities. The Qur'anic verses acknowledge and celebrate the presence of sexuality in all of humankind because we are created as sexual beings and very quickly understand the power of the sexual impulse. Indeed, Ghazali argued that God was capable of creating humans without sexual desire and the need for human sexual organs to reproduce. Since he had not, and sexual desire was as an inescapable feature of human minds and bodies, there can be nothing wrong in exercising our sexuality.[6] Yet it is precisely because it is so powerful that sexual relations are commended within licit frameworks and limited by moral scruples.

Regulation is described through categorisation of relationships in which marriage remains the most significant. Indeed the Qur'an refers to male–female relationships most often in the context of marriage. Marriage is judged in Islamic thought to be the fundamental basis of a moral society, providing the framework for personal and social wellbeing and even happiness. Despite long discourses about marriage in theological works, marriage is encouraged though not obligatory in the Qur'an. According to some prophetic hadiths, marriage is equivalent to having one half of faith, the Prophet stating that those who do not marry are not from his followers.[7]

The juristic literature of the Islamic world saw marriage principally through negotiated rights and obligations because marriage was seen as a contract. Fundamentally the term *nikah* implies a legal contract between a man and a woman, a social institution and the physical act of sexual intercourse. While marriage is always more than the legitimisation of sexual intercourse, the fundamental premise of *nikah* is that it validates intercourse between male and female so that marriage and coitus are linked. Thus, legally the marriage contract makes operative sense only when sexual intercourse between the husband and wife can take place, and it is only upon this union that so many of the rights and duties between husband and wife in a marriage are premised. Marriage is referred to in various contexts in the Qur'an, with the following verses the most commonly used in reference to the subject:

> And among His signs is this, that He created for you mates from among yourselves, that you may dwell in tranquillity with them, and He has put love and mercy between your hearts. Undoubtedly in these are signs for those who reflect. (Q30:21)

Thus, the Qur'an is clear that it is God who places love and mercy between the couple, so that they find repose in each other. However, verses of love and repose are not common in the Qur'an, for marital love is very rarely mentioned. The Qur'an is not a book of love stories. Human love is always mentioned in the context of a love which is essentially above passion and feeling, beyond the poetic. Rather, it is about commitment, doing and fidelity. To love, therefore, is to have intentions and engagement towards another person. The ideal love in marriage or between two people is always based on compassion and mutual responsibilities. The Qur'an affirms human sexual needs and sees marriage as a desirable and permissible remedy for natural passions. This is a world which divides society between the pre-pubescent and the post-pubescent, in which the latter become eligible to marry and thereby express sexual need.

While Islamic cultures vigorously extol the virtue and importance of marriage, there is no command to marry in the Qur'an itself, even if there is a strong directive in both the Qur'an and the hadith literature that marriage is a desirable and practicable state for a good Islamic life. While the Qur'an addresses the question of those for whom marriage is and is not permitted, the closest we get to an actual encouragement to marry is contained in the verse 'You shall encourage those of you who are single to get married' (Q24:32). It is only within the wider field of Islamic discourse that the virtues and pleasures of marriage are discussed. Sexual need, particularly male sexual desire, is considered a dominant reason for marrying, as sexual desire is too powerful an impulse and too great a distraction from service to God. In his section on the benefits of marriage, Ghazali writes that one of the benefits of marriage is that is protects against the 'dangers of lust'.[8] In Ghazali's view, man has been created weak and cannot be patient when it comes to women. He refers to Junaid the Sufi who is reported as having said, '"Sexual intercourse is as necessary for me like food is necessary for me" and indeed the wife is strictly speaking nourishment and the reason for the purity of the heart.'[9] In an age of increased equality and shared roles between men and women, speaking of the wife as nourishment may sound demeaning to women. But the Qur'an and other genres of classical Islamic literature reflect largely patriarchal contexts. Here, male and female desire are equally recognised but, as so often in religious literature, it is the male voice we hear. The view of women seen as nourishment and temptation is a theme that is repeated, but one that is not exclusive to the Islamic tradition. While celibacy is of no particular significance in Islam, it can be found in various ascetic movements throughout Islamic history. For many of the Sufis, male lust and sexual desire was a particular problem if it led you away from reflection on God. Thus, we find in the celebrated Arabic work of the tenth-century al-Makki the legitimate pathways of both marriage and celibacy:

> God, may he be praised, has decreed neither marriage nor celibacy, just as he has not made it a duty that every man marry four women. But he has decreed integrity of heart, preservation

of faith, a soul at peace, and the execution of commands needed for these. If one's rectitude resides in marriage then that is better for him. If one's uprightness and peacefulness of soul exist with four women, then it is allowable for him to seek his peace and a healthy disposition as long as he fulfills the obligatory conditions. If one is content with one woman then that one is better and more preferred for him since she is more appropriate for his wellbeing. And if one's healthful condition, integrity of heart, and peace of soul reside in celibacy then that is better for him, since these are the things that are desired of marriage. If one can reach these without marriage then celibacy causes no harm.[10]

But sexual fulfilment in marriage is affirmed for both men and women. There is no shame in sex, there is no shame in desire, and both men and women have rights over one another. Romantic love and sex may not be the same thing, but marriage should have both. When sexual desire is realised in marriage, one is acting according to a traditional Islamic understanding of how *eros* finds its place in human life.

The Qur'an sees marriage as good for both sexes, but directs itself to men, stating that men can marry 'women of their choice' (Q4:3). This recognition also extends to encouraging masters to arrange marriages for their slaves and slave girls. There is a Qur'anic verse which is explicit in urging restraint in circumstances: 'Let those who cannot afford to marry keep themselves chaste until God enriches them from his bounty' (Q24:33). The financial aspect of marriage is therefore inextricably tied with human sexual desire. A prophetic hadith also emphasises the importance of marriage as a relationship for fulfilling sexual needs and thus avoiding immodest and lewd behaviour: 'Whoever is able to marry should marry for that will help him lower his gaze and guard his private parts [from committing illicit sexual intercourse].'[11] This may come across as almost quaint in its tone, yet marriage is not just about the fulfilment of sexual desire; it is also about the fidelity and personal modesty which accompanies this mutual commitment. The mention of the lowered gaze and guarding private parts indicates that marriage is an ideal where both partners find solace in each other, thus minimising carnal urges for anyone else. Much of Islamic poetic literature concerns itself with the gaze or the look between two people, as it is the glance of desire which projects the being of one person into the consciousness of another. In his analysis of sexual desire, Roger Scruton writes:

> And this glance is compromising: for it seeks a response from a free being, who may withhold it indignantly, or who may return a glance of his own. And to return the glance is to acquiesce. The glance asks *you* to respond to *me*. I am inevitably held to account for it and while I may excuse myself on account of the strength of my passion, the last thing I want is for you to take that excuse seriously, to see me subdued by desire as by an alien force, rather than riding towards you triumphantly upon a crest of feeling that I also control.[12]

Scruton argues that it is the eye which enables the human person to be revealed to another in his body, to 'look out' of his body and 'in the act of revelation to summon the other's perspective, in the form of blushes, smiles or a reciprocated glance'.[13]

While Islamic literature is reflective of Islamic societies in portraying all kinds of sexual relationships, there has been a tendency to regard marriage as the only faithful context for a sexual life. The complexity of human desire has been lost in the insistence that heterosexual marriage alone provides the divinely sanctioned context for a sexual life. It is marriage which creates the context in which two people can share the mutuality of physical and emotional needs, and thus marriage without consummation, without the mutual enjoyment of sex, has no real place in Islam. Love in its carnal form transforms our being, and men and women are seen as impotent without each other.

Although much of the jurisprudential debate on marriage in Islam looked at the sexual and contractual nature of this union, Islamic discussions of marriage in the classical and modern period have generally focused on faithful marriage as essential to family life and societal good. Thus, marriage is seen as containing both personal and societal benefits. Muslim writers have often placed in diametric opposition Qur'anic affirmation and fulfilment of sexual desire as intrinsic to the human condition and patriarchal expressions of Islam that deny women their spiritual and legal equality. They argue that Islam recognises and celebrates human sexuality in both men and women, gives them rights over each other whilst creating a legal framework for lawful sex. To be human is to desire, and human sexuality is seen as one of our greatest driving impulses. This impulse, which can bring both solace and temptation, should not be denied, but this impulse must also bear a moral and legal outcome. For marriage to be a force for good in society it must also remain a moral commitment, and the marriage ceremony and institutional customs are a public endorsement of an exclusive privacy and an exclusive bond. The *nikah*, therefore, is not just a vow between two people but a public acknowledgement. The importance of marriage as a public event, validated by the onlooker, is established across cultures. Scruton argues that the obligations of private love are protected through the institution of marriage and that social existence is 'existence under observation'. He writes:

If we develop the capacity for the vow of love, it is because we see ourselves reflected in this public observation, as objects of judgement that can make no exceptions in their own favour … The public pressure on the individual is made bearable by marriage, which instructs others to avert their eyes and to create the legitimacy of a life lived privately. This division between the public and the private creates the private, by creating the space from which others are excluded.[14]

Sexual transgression, therefore, goes against the personal integrity of both parties, rejects the social worth of marriage and ultimately rejects the transcendent realm of God's desired order. Notwithstanding the imperative of sexual union, marriage requires more than the ability and willingness to consummate the union, and it is here that one can explore and emphasise the variety of human emotions which keep a marriage together. In his seminal work *Sexuality in Islam*, Bouhdiba discusses at length the centrality but ambivalent dimensions of sex and sexuality in Islam, which he describes as the 'serious and the ludic, the social and the individual, the sacramental and the historical'. Bouhdiba explains:

Through sexuality the whole human being is taken seriously. This is why so much attention is paid to sexuality. Sexuality is to be taken seriously because it bears witness to the seriousness of existence … One should marry. One should have sexual intercourse. Parents must marry off their children and among the duties of filial piety is that of getting a widowed parent to remarry.[15]

In another Qur'anic verse, husband and wife are likened to garments for one another (Q2:187). The implication here is one of mutual dignity and also of protection, where each is responsible to the other. Garments cover, beautify and signify closeness to the flesh. They can of course reveal and conceal, hide and allure, and sexuality is always present in this image. But in a religion where clothing has for many retained a central place in defining the ideal image of Muslim piety and modesty, the concept of husband and wife being garments for one another is a potent and demanding depiction of complementarity. Marriage is a guardian of modesty for both. Thus, if sexuality is central to the Muslim understanding of the self and conjugal relationships, so is modesty. The affirmation of sexuality and the sexual impulse is implicit in the marriage contract, but so too is the recognition that the sexual exists within the ethics of modesty. Modesty and sexuality contain a certain even paradoxical sacrality in the Islamic tradition, as both are regarded as fundamental to the ideal of an Islamic society. Muslim writers often use these verses to argue that marriage is more than a legal contract in Islam and that it is in fact an act of worship which enables physical and spiritual fulfilment between the spouses.

Every human relationship is vulnerable and tested in life. We need to cultivate a level of self-discipline and love to keep our relationships strong. Whether people are drawn to or bound in relationships by birth or by choice, relationships need a level of commitment which goes beyond just subjective feeling towards one another. We can have feelings for many people in our lives, including deep longing, but marriage must be based on mutual fidelity and the mutual desire to keep the relationship meaningful. It is too easy to stop caring, to drift apart and to hope that one day someone more ideal will come along. Most marriages will go through these phases, even those marriages where there is love and respect. I think this is precisely why there is a strong theme of mutual rights and obligations running throughout the Qur'an when referring to relationships and also to family and social ties in general. The onus is on people to understand and fulfil their commitments to the best of their abilities, irrespective of how they might actually feel about one another. Faith in God is reflected in faith in one another.

However we cultivate these disciplines, there is a passage in the Qur'an which illustrates the combination of virtues expected in the ideal Muslim, whether male or female:

> Indeed, the Muslim men and Muslim women, the believing men and believing women, the obedient men and obedient women, the truthful men and truthful women, the patient men and patient women, the humble men and humble women, the charitable men and charitable women, the fasting men and fasting women, the men who guard their private parts and the women who do so, and the men who remember Allah often and the women who do so – for them Allah has prepared forgiveness and a great reward. (Q33:35)

Gender egalitarianism may be interpreted in the cultivation of certain characteristics including patience, obedience and humility. The guarding of private parts is repeated throughout the Qur'an as extolling a specific virtue which sits ethically alongside other Qur'anic exhortations such as remembrance of God. Thus, sexual virtue and piety seem to be inextricably linked. The taxonomy of actions which places fasting, remembrance of God and 'guarding of private parts' in the same category reflects a particular ethics in which the boundaries between the earthly and the transcendent come together in the virtue ethics of the Qur'an. Performing rituals such as fasting, remembering God and retaining chaste behaviour are all aspects of worship, and worship is always understood in the context of humility before God. Worship of God entails being and living in a certain way and where formal religious ritual is just one aspect of that devotion to God. There is an acknowledgement made in the Qur'an that certain ways of being are good and the cultivation and preservation of such characteristics is what God likes in humankind. Extolling concepts such as chastity as a religious virtue and thus a virtuous way of being for the believer may sound like common sense in most religious traditions, but chaste behaviour in both men and women is one of the biggest demands made on us. By chastity I don't simply mean refraining from sexual relations before marriage and outside of marriage. Rather, I define chastity like modesty, fundamental in all human relationships, a willingness to resist relenting to any desire that is unlawful. This is hard because our lives are full of moments which challenge our certainties, loyalties and faith.

The Qur'an is not a compendium to the ideal marriage. It provides certain principles which have been elaborated in the various intellectual disciplines of Islam. While principles of mutual fidelity and trust and sexual fulfilment are intrinsic to a good marriage, there is no sense that marriage is a guarantee of human happiness or the solution to the quest for fulfilled lives. Marriages can be painful and bring misery and divorce, and other forms of separation exist in Islam as a recognition of broken relationships. In my view it is precisely because the Qur'an recognises that marriage creates a faithful context but cannot limit human desire, that it doesn't stigmatise divorce but provides the skeletal framework for dissolving the contract.

Yet divorce is a difficult concept even today within many Muslim families. When I was growing up, I can't remember any of my parents' friends or any of my own relatives being divorced. Divorce was like a taboo word: it was hardly mentioned, and when the word did occasionally come up, the atmosphere was solemn. It was as if respectable people neither divorced nor talked of divorce. Yet as Rapoport writes, contrary to modern assumptions based on an ideological framework of the past, divorce was common in medieval Middle East societies:

> If the family was indeed the central building block of pre-modern Muslim society, and an institution that was to be protected from the penetrating eyes of the public gaze, then we should expect the incidence of divorce to be as low as possible. Indeed, if the ideal family of medieval Muslims societies was the patriarchal household, frequent divorce would surely have resulted in the creation of familial institutions that were less than ideal, as many more women would have had to make a living on their own. Moreover, if medieval Muslim societies looked upon the unattached young female as a threat to morality, and if marriage was so highly prized for both men and women, we would expect to find divorce being used only as a last resort. This was clearly not the case for much of the history of the Islamic Middle-East.[16]

However terrible divorce is viewed in traditional society, it is treated as the end of a contract in the manuals of classical Islamic jurisprudence. Its personal dimension is left unexplored. But in the words of the German cultural theorist and philosopher Theodor Adorno, we find a description that we will all recognise. Adorno writes that even between good-natured and educated people, divorce stirs up a dust cloud 'that covers and discolours all it touches'. Intimacy and trust disappear because the relationship is now broken. Adorno states that in a divorce, 'things which were once signs of loving care, signs of reconciliation, breaking loose as independent values, show their evil, cold and pernicious side'.[17] All that was once protected is now cruelly exposed. It would seem that much of human unhappiness is caused by people feeling trapped within relationships, including marriage. I remember speaking with an American Christian colleague who had divorced from his wife after many years, despite not wishing to initiate a divorce. He revealed the many years of unhappiness he had endured, but also why he felt it was wrong to divorce. My reply was that no marriage could last if there was only unhappiness; there had to be some moments of happiness. He answered in almost a mocking tone: 'That's not true, I know so many couples who live miserable lives but pretend to be happy.' This may sound familiar to many people, but there is something uniquely sad about the human search for happiness and fulfilment in one another and the despair which often meets us.

When I reflect on my own life, and the cultural context in which marriages were for the most part arranged, I am aware that our lives are intertwined with competing loyalties to family, religion and tradition. We were a family of three brothers and three sisters growing up in a Muslim home. My mother wanted successful careers for us above all, but also suitable husbands for the girls – and in her mind a suitable husband was preferably an arranged husband. I didn't mind this as long as I had a say. When I tell people today, most are genuinely surprised – the whole system seems so archaic to them. They see it as a clash of different modernities and are surprised that my faith has been a constant guide as well as a challenge, especially when the narrative of the modern age is so heavily focused on individualism and personal choice.

It is difficult to think of the precise moment when you discover that you are no longer what you thought you were and that the change has been gradual not sudden. I remember the very first time I went abroad on my own as an undergraduate. I had travelled to Cairo for the first time to learn Arabic and my parents had been happy to send me there on my own because it was for the sake of my education. I was never afraid of travelling on my own and even though I was 20 or 21 years of age, I was confident about who I was and what I believed. My mother had simply said, 'Always remember who you are.' I felt sure that I would enjoy my time as a young Muslim woman who was entering a new adventure and all too aware that the best part of any journey is the element of surprise.

When I studied in Cairo, I became close friends with an Australian diplomat who was slightly older than me and in the year above me, where students learnt advanced Arabic. All the students had their breaks at the same time and we would all mingle as the 'English speakers'. He often teased me for my peculiar mix of naivite and confidence, based on an upbringing that had created the kind of boundaries in which I felt safe – even though part of me wanted to escape. I lived at a distance from where I could observe the world and the lives people led, yet always remained emotionally uninvolved. He often told me I had 'spunk', a word with which I was unfamiliar at the time but that I later understood was meant as a compliment. I liked him for understanding me, disagreeing with me, but always respecting my religious faith. Our conversations about life and relationships drew me closer to him, while all the time I kept wondering what boundaries I was crossing. Every friendship was platonic and I realised that that was not the way most people thought of male–female relationships. But my upbringing and my faith were part of who I was, and the distance from family and familiarity only convinced me that I was confident with the boundaries I had set myself, no matter how close I felt to someone. I made many friends while I was there, but I particularly enjoyed the closeness of this friendship. When I was leaving to return to the UK, we said goodbye and as we did, he leant over to give me a hug. I remember recoiling, thoroughly embarrassed and ashamed of myself. How had I given such an impression, where a man felt he was at liberty to show me physical affection, even if it was just a friendly hug? It sounds so innocent, and looking back I sound so immature, but there are times when you know you have discovered something about yourself which you can't quite identify straightaway. On my return flight I kept thinking about why I had recoiled when I felt so comfortable with him. I realised that I wanted all the experiences of life without feeling unsettled and that was impossible. I was a different person now.

Being desired and desiring another is one of the most intriguing aspects of growing up and getting to know oneself, but a commitment like marriage involves so many considerations. In my background, marriage wasn't simply an individual choice borne of love or attraction, but a collective decision where social standing, education, wealth and religion matter – and matter to the whole family. My mother didn't talk much about marriage, but in the few discussions we had, I sensed that my parents had given us many freedoms but always with the hope that we would not defy certain customs and traditions. So I knew that should there be any serious clash of views between myself and my mother, I would give in. I was rather fatalistic at times, hoping that obedience carried its own rewards and that duty to parents was a greater virtue, often eclipsing individual choice. In arranged marriages, happiness is assumed as an inevitable consequence of parental choice. Compatibility is chiefly measured according to background, education and wealth; the meeting of minds is left to chance. But it seems to me that it is precisely in the meeting of minds and intellectual intimacy that true happiness lies.

In recent years there has been some criticism of this modern stress on intimacy as a fundamental requirement of happiness. Christopher Lasch critiques the 'cult of intimacy' between men and women, which he argues 'conceals a growing despair of finding it'. Personal relations crumble under this emotional weight.[18] Yet, it seems that despite the elusive nature of so much that we search for in life, men and women continue to find richness and intensity in this quest.

In some ways I made sense of an arranged marriage by having faith in God, believing that there would be a good and happy outcome if I continued to trust God, try to be a loving wife and be patient and confident. I didn't want to feel that I had settled nor did I ever wish that for my husband, and so I immersed myself fully into this new relationship which I knew simply had to work because it was now my life and my future. I would often remind myself and my husband that happiness was not some state to which we could simply lift ourselves; it needed work, it needed mutual connection. Like most marriages, there have been moments of reflection, questions asked, but I realised very early on that for marriage to be good for the body and the soul, it needs joy. Loving and being loved is not an intellectual pursuit, it isn't about rights and duties, it isn't about the contract on which marriage is premised – it is simply about feeling and doing for one another. I remember reading for the first time the following lines from Milan Kundera's *The Unbearable Lightness of Being*:

Perhaps all the questions we ask of love, to measure, test, probe, and save it, have the additional effect of cutting it short. Perhaps the reason we are unable to love is that we yearn to be loved, that is, we demand something (love) from our partner instead of delivering ourselves up to him demand-free and asking for nothing but his company.[19]

Kundera points to the common human error which destroys so many relationships – our fear of being vulnerable, and a false pride. Love holds an endless fragility yet it is at the same time about holding onto the heavy, the difficult, knowing that two people are unfolding their worlds within themselves and for one another. What I have come to realise over the years in my own marriage is that there is no room for false pride and that love has to be given before it is received. By this I don't mean that there is no place for self-respect, but the kind of pride that destroys human empathy confuses love with mere sentiment. Love demands both courage and humility, and effective communication means you have to listen well, understand what someone else wants, not what you think they want. When two people commit to each other, choose to live together, they need a level of humility to reach out to one another, be the first to break the silence. Silence in a marriage is the worst kind of silence. It is only by physically breaking the silence that we can show once again that we care about the relationship, we care about each other and are willing to talk, to love, forgive and be forgiven. A marriage can't survive without the element of forgiveness because it is in forgiveness that we reveal human compassion and human want. It is in those moments of forgiveness, whether we are close or distant, that we grow as people and learn how to love.

When we first married, my husband would say that he was raised never to have high expectations of other people:

the less you expected, the less you were disappointed. There was a certain stoicism to this outlook, with which I always disagreed. I argued that a husband and wife should have expectations of each another. In this most intimate and often intense relationship, both should be open and feel that the other is to some extent accountable for their mutual happiness. If I couldn't have expectations of my husband, who else would I turn to? It isn't that we should expect one person to fill our lives with everything, but nor can we live meaningfully with too many voids. I have been married for over 22 years now and if I was to distil three important elements to a happy marriage, a good marriage, they would be mutual respect, mutual desire and the willingness and courage to take the relationship seriously without taking oneself too seriously. Marriage, like most love relationships, is not a charity; rather, it is built on reciprocity. A husband and wife should always nurture hopes in one another because this balances the giving and the taking, wanting and being wanted; this reciprocity is a gift in marriage.

Although the prophets and sages talk of real happiness only in spiritual terms, that it is to be found in the pursuit and worship of God, human happiness is important in this life. It can be found in many of life's riches, but there is no weakness in associating a level of our happiness with other people. In the end it may be true, as Emerson says, that 'nothing can bring you happiness but yourself', but a good marriage can bring joy to our lives and still remains fundamental to the way many people conceptualise their personal happiness. I don't interpret happiness as being in a constant state of bliss or even believe that happiness is the real purpose of life, but I do feel that an unhappy life is not a well-lived life.

To live life well we need to be conscious and intelligent with our emotions and be able to feel and sense the world with all its possibilities. In his reflections on happiness, the Turkish Nobel laureate Orhan Pamuk writes:

> Is it vulgar to be happy? I've often wondered about this. Now I think about it all the time. Even though I have said that people who are capable are evil and stupid, from time to time I think this too: no, to be happy is not rude, and it takes brains.[20]

There are too many people who live with unhappiness but security, as if the latter cancels out the former. In the 1970s, Christopher Lasch criticised the jaded appetites of the average Americans whom he considered lived submissive and bland lives. Lasch wrote:

> Twentieth century peoples have erected so many psychological barriers against strong emotion, and have invested those defences with so much of the energy derived from forbidden impulse, that they can no longer remember what it feels like to be inundated by desire.[21]

It is also true that when someone asks us 'Are you a happy?', most of us don't immediately say 'Yes' or 'No', but pause, however briefly, to give some thought to our response, knowing that this question more than many others takes us deeper into ourselves. On the one hand, we have the philosophical explanations which define happiness as elusive, or the Kantian approach in which it is a virtue to want happiness for others, but wanting happiness for oneself, which is based on self-love, can never be a virtue. On the other hand, the growing force of the media forever tells us that happiness is within our reach. Scott Peck argues with wit and poignancy that the biggest lie sold to us is that we are meant to be happy all the time:

> We're bombarded by business, the media, and the church with the lie that we're here to be happy, fulfilled, and comfortable. For motives of profit, the lies of materialism and advertising suggest that if we're not happy, comfortable, and fulfilled, we must be eating the wrong cereal or driving the wrong car. Or that we must not have it right with God. How wicked! The truth is our finest moments, more often than not, occur precisely when we are uncomfortable, when we're not feeling happy or fulfilled, when we're struggling and searching.[22]

However subjective happiness is, and however difficult it is to measure, feeling happy must be based on at least a minimal sense that life is worth living and that we are not alone. Thus it is only when we read accounts of a person's deep unhappiness, that we begin to understand how disabling and how destructive the sense of loneliness is to a person's sense of wellbeing. In her acclaimed journals, Sylvia Plath describes the intensity of her own loneliness:

> God, but life is loneliness, despite all the opiates, despite the shrill tinsel gaiety of 'parties' with no purpose, despite the soft grinning faces we all wear. And when at last you find someone to whom you feel you can pour out your soul, you stop in shock at the words you utter – they are so rusty so ugly, so meaningless and feeble from being kept in the small cramped dark inside you so long. Yes, there is joy, fulfilment and companionship – but the loneliness of the soul in its appealing self-consciousness, is horrible and overpowering.[23]

As my own children reach adulthood, I think about their futures and the choices they will make in their lives, especially when it comes to marriage. Theirs is a generation where friendships are central to happiness, but they too are carrying within their lives some of the charms and tensions of being part of two cultures. I count myself lucky that I have grown up in the liberal, social milieu of a Western society where I've enjoyed the freedom to resist the more rigorist conceptions of some Muslims that Muslims cannot be true friends with non-Muslims, that a shared faith should be a defining premise of any friendship. This freedom is both a virtue and a privilege because it is not universal. It has left me convinced that my faith in God has been strengthened by some of the soul searching I have done over friends. In a way, the history of my friendships has been a journey of faith as well. It has made me think about those who have brought out the best in me, unsettled me or challenged my faith.

When I look at the way my children interact with their friends, I realise so much has changed in one generation. I have thought much about this over the last few years, as I see my children turn into young adults. They haven't had the experience of living as part of an extended family system or even growing up under the watchful and protective gaze of my parents, their grandparents. In a way, that has been a loss but also allowed for a greater freedom of thought and expression. Young people have a way of finding their independence whatever their upbringing. My children enjoy an even greater freedom, and for them their friends are like an extended family. Their close friendships with boys and girls of various backgrounds have, I think, made them more open and generous, more sympathetic young citizens and prompts me to think of my own life and those who came and went. I do believe that we are shaped emotionally and intellectually by those who touch our lives and who we allow to stay in our lives. I wasn't attracted to piety but rather to generosity, and realise that I forgave much if it came with a big heart. I didn't search for Muslim friends and South Asian friends, but seemed to respond only to those who understood something of me. It is precisely because friendship involves risks and takes us away from the comfort of religious and psychological convictions, forcing us to ponder on life's uncertainties and ambiguities, that friendships can become defining points in our lives.

When we talk of marriage, my children appreciate that love, sex and marriage are serious matters, that leading a moral life is a serious matter, but they also know they are free to decide on such issues. These are some of the most important decisions we make in life, the decisions which can bring us levels of both happiness and unhappiness. I feel that too many parents who have lovingly supported their children in other areas of their lives, insist on infantilising their adult sons and daughters when it comes to marriage. The overwhelming desire to hold onto family ties and certain traditions can often ignore what the children themselves desire; love and cultural and intellectual compatibility aren't sacrificed – they're often simply dismissed. Traditions are important because they can give you a sense of history and continuity, but most young people nowadays want to understand first, rather than just follow. I pray that they find love in their lives and that they continue to believe in God, because both love and faith bring mystery and depth to our lives. The passion the young feel for wanting is endearing but misplaced. They also need to appreciate that finding and holding onto both love and faith require patience. Reading Rilke's *Letters to a Young Poet* one afternoon, I came across one of his most famous passages which encapsulates some of what I feel:

> You are so young, all still lies ahead of you, and I should like to ask you, as best I can, dear Sir, to be patient towards all that is unresolved in your heart and to try to love the questions themselves like locked rooms, like books written in a foreign tongue. Do not strive to uncover answers: they cannot be given you because you have not been able to live them. And what matters is to live the questions for now. Perhaps then you will gradually, without noticing it, live your way into the answer, one distant day in the future.[24]

It is important that we give our children a level of independence but that we continue to guide them, to tell them that there are ways of living well, ways of living with the questions of life; not everything has an answer, but a meaningful life is one which continues to enjoy this search. This is a struggle today, where the hallmark of society is so often based on consumerism and instantaneous satisfaction, immediate answers, a society which 'promises to take the waiting out of wanting, sweat out of effort and effort out of results'.[25] But young people need to know and see that there is an art to everything in life, including the art of loving and living, where both require courage, patience and discipline.

Over the years I have seen many arranged marriages and know that finding suitable partners for your children is not easy. There are parents today who are struggling not to find an 'ideal partner' for their child but just a 'suitable partner'. Most Muslim societies still hold onto certain principles of arranged marriages even when living in the West. They realise that they must be more flexible, more accommodating to their children's desires, but parents want to stay involved as much as possible. In one generation, I realise that my personal views on so many aspects of my children's lives have become very different from those around me. The young people of today are global citizens, more travelled and experienced than those of a generation ago. Alongside this experience, technology connects them to a wider world where they can see for themselves the injustices and complexities of life. They may harbour a certain innocence, but they are aware and far more confident about questioning what they don't understand and what they find hypocritical. For many, religious faith promises hope but gives few answers to their most immediate concerns.

Here, that most central and intimate relationship, marriage, proves a particular challenge for understanding relationships and fidelity. I say this with specific reference to marriage in Muslim societies. The issue of chastity and abstinence before marriage may be a pious ideal, but Islamic history and contemporary Islamic societies show that it remains just that – an ideal. Many are oblivious to the complex history of sex and sexuality in Islamic societies. In his recent work on sexual desire in the Arab world, Joseph Massad surveys a wide variety of literature, including the psychoanalytical, to show how Arabs represented their own sexual desires. Massad portrays a variety of sexual behaviour practised in Arab societies and in literature, challenging Western binary perceptions of either licentiousness or prudishness. While Arab is not the same as Islamic, Abdelwahab Bouhdiba's sophisticated work also argues how the openness of an original Islam was corrupted by the practice of the segregation of the sexes, which led to an exaltation of promiscuity:

It is difficult for those who have not experienced it to imagine
what life under a strict separation of the sexes is like. But it is
understandable that homosexuality, so violently condemned by
Islam, could be so widely practised among both men and women
... The fact that homosexuality was always being condemned
proves only one thing: neither the religious nor the social
conscience could put an end to practices that were disapproved of
by Islamic ethics, but to which in the last resort society closed it
eyes. Cousinage, prostitution, amorous intrigues of all kinds were
inadequate to cope with the expression of desires that turned
quite 'naturally' to homosexuality.[26]

Bouhdiba argues that the sexual ethic experienced by Muslims
and the vision of the world that underlies it have less and
less to do with the generous declarations of the Qur'an and
Muhammad himself. He writes: 'One can even speak of a
degradation, which began at a very early date, of an ideal
model. The open sexuality practised in joy with a view to the
fulfilment of being, gradually gave way to a closed, morose,
repressed sexuality.'[27]

Today, many have begun to rethink how we define the
significance of abstention and chastity, knowing that there
exists a huge gulf between a particular ideal of abstention and
virtue and the reality of sexual desire prevalent in all human
beings. Sexual mores were complex in the past and they
have become even more complex today. In modern societies,
where women and men of all backgrounds enjoy a much
greater array of freedoms than was possible only a couple
of generations ago, attitudes to sex and relationships have
changed enormously everywhere, and especially in the West
where cultural theorists analyse the effects of our changed
lifestyles and expectations. Zygmunt Bauman comments on
the isolation of sex from love, this most fundamental change
which defines our liquid societies:

Sex is now expected to be self sustained and self sufficient, to 'stand on its own feet', to be judged solely by the satisfaction it may bring on its own (even if it stops as a rule well short of the expectations beefed up by the media). No wonder that its capacity to spawn frustration, and to exacerbate the very same sensation of estrangement it was hoped to heal, has also grown enormously. Sex's victory in the great war of independence has been, in the best of circumstances, pyrrhic. The wonder drug appears to produce ailments and sufferings no less numerous and arguably more acute than those it promised to cure.[28]

Bauman quotes a short anecdote from the therapist Volkmar Sigusch, who records the complaints and grievances of people who are the casualties of this kind of 'pure sex':

All forms of intimate relationships currently in vogue bear the same mask of false happiness once worn by marital and later by free love ... As we took a closer look and pulled away the mask, we found unfulfilled yearnings, ragged nerves, disappointed love, hurts, fears, loneliness, hypocrisy, egotism and repetition compulsion ... Performances have replaced ecstasy, physics are in, metaphysics out ... Abstinence, monogamy, and promiscuity are all equally far removed from the free life of sensuality that none of us knows.[29]

As the mystery of sex has gone, the yearning for meaningful relationships has increased. Sex has become loaded with too many expectations for human fulfilment, beyond its capacity to deliver. In this vein, Christopher Lasch argues that sex valued purely for its own sake loses all reference to the future, bringing no hope of permanent relationships:

The demystification of womanhood goes hand in hand with the desublimation of sexuality ... Institutionalised sexual segregation has given way to arrangements that promote the intermingling of the sexes at every stage of life. Efficient contraceptives, legalised abortion, and a 'realistic' and 'healthy' acceptance of the body have weakened the links that once tied sex to love, marriage, and procreation. Men and women now pursue sexual pleasure as an end in itself, unmediated even by the conventional trappings of romance.[30]

In many Islamic contexts, it is this phenomenon of unfulfilled lives which free sex produces that has to be avoided. In this fervour there is an unwillingness to think through the complexity of the human condition, including addressing the issue of secrecy around sexual relations between young people. Rather, sexual freedom and the gradual change in attitudes have been accompanied by an even greater desire amongst some, especially in the West, to emphasise an ethos of male–female segregation. It is as if physical segregation is an answer to every social problem or emotional crisis. Segregation between the sexes has in recent times become a common phenomenon at many social events and where clothing, both through the wearing of the *hijab/niqab*, expresses a seemingly unquestionable piety. Here I would like to make one thing clear. I am sure that covering for some women is an act of faith, a real expression of their piety notwithstanding issues about peer or parental pressure and debates on religious identity. However, I am concerned that covering in this particular way deflects from so many other serious, even painful issues which have beset these communities, thus hindering social and moral progress. Clothing has become a marker of identity, but in emphasising an Islamic otherness, it has also created a culture of defensiveness and insularity.

The call to engage men and women together to understand the challenges of diverse and mixed societies, where human loneliness and need for security requires an array of responses, is either ignored or muted and physical segregation extolled as the ultimate religious imperative and social value. A failure to understand that chastity and modesty aren't intrinsically tied to segregation has created an anomalous atmosphere where people are free to mix in public life but often segregated in the privacy of their own home cultures. Where segregation is not possible, the wearing of the *hijab* or *niqab* is seen as a desirable and necessary alternative since, according to some, it functions as a form of portable segregation.[31] I believe that modesty and honour are quite central to an Islamic ethic, but much of the contemporary debate has limited the very concept of modesty to gender segregation alone, where women continue to be the primary repositories of sexual ethics and family values. Thus, as people's lives have become more complex in relation to all kinds of issues around gender and rights, the solutions have been simplified often to the point of absurdity. Dress and segregation are projected as the answer to all problems. My purpose is not to repeat the endless religious arguments which are for or against the wearing of the headcovering or the face covering, but to question the reasons for this rising trend. Personally speaking, there appears to be an obsession with dress among many Muslim communities as the defining image of the modern and practising Muslim.

Over the last couple of decades I have often found myself as the only woman, maybe one of a handful, at an event or gathering in the UK, Europe and North America, whose head hasn't been covered. This is not a political stance, but dress has become a politicised issue. I am also aware that by choosing not to cover in this way, I am an easy target for many Muslims who consider me too secular or even immodest to be part of the debate on Islam. This is their prerogative of course, and equally I am often asked by non-Muslim audiences why I dress in a 'Westernised' way and how that affects my standing within Muslim societies. I find these questions tedious and presumptive, but the popular image of Islam in the West is one in which female dress matters. Muslim women are so often the victims of injustice and abuse of rights in different parts of the world, that to reduce gender relations to the specifics of dress is in my view very unfortunate. It seems to me that unless Muslims are willing to actively engage with pluralism in all matters of life and religion, debates on Islam and the place of Islam as a public and private faith will continue to remain for the most part simplistic and uninspiring.

The paradox of the *hijab* and *niqab* is that they are seen by some as the ultimate signs of modesty, but they can only hide so much. As human beings, we all share similar desires but we also share the responsibility to meet the true complexities of life and not to reduce life to simple do's and don'ts. Covering has become synonymous with modesty so that hardly anyone questions the behaviour or language of those who are covered. This curious phenomenon has halted the exploration of how women can continue to uphold certain moral norms which they associate with their Islamic faith while living relatively freer lives than their parents. Several years ago, a Muslim woman academic working at a senior level at a British university commented that one of her biggest frustrations in recent times was the increasing use of the *niqab* by young Muslims girls who were in her opinion actually leading double lives. Her argument was that the *niqab* had become such a potent expression of piety that some Muslim communities were turning a blind eye to the actual behaviour of so many young women. She added, 'So many come to my office and do you know what they ask for? They ask for the morning after pill. What kind of society are we creating where so much is hidden behind the *niqab*?' She spoke in a calm manner, like someone who had been dealing with this for a long time, but her concerns about this kind of lifestyle and life circumstances ran deep. We both reflected on the cultural even spiritual vacuum that had encouraged so many young women to follow such directions in life. It was not as if many of the young women felt liberated or empowered through their sexual experiences; they were simply lost or lonely and their faith could not provide any answers. The need for men and women holding authority in their communities to speak up about such issues with compassion and understanding, not judgement and contempt, has gained a new urgency.

A recent conversation with a Muslim woman brings to the surface some of the challenges Muslims face today in their appraisal of what it means to live the good life, especially when it comes to issues of marriage and family. Where traditionally the exhortations within the Qur'an and *sunna*, the customs and expectations of most Islamic societies, all point to marriage as an absolute foundation in the life of the good Muslim, the rise of divorce, separation and other forms of marital breakdowns has led many to question the continuing centrality of marriage as a virtue in Muslim life. This is especially so in relation to the traditional form of arranged marriages, which remains the most popular, albeit at times contested, practice of marriage amongst many Muslims.

The woman in question, a medical doctor by profession, had lived most of her life in the USA and divorced several years earlier. She was visiting the UK with her children and grandchildren to attend her niece's wedding. As she looked around the wedding hall she expressed some reservations about the financial expense of contemporary weddings and added, 'All this is just show to fill up our time; we are born alone and we die lone, that is the only reality.' I wasn't sure whether this comment was just an expression of her own marital experience, a certain sorrow at the breakdown of her marriage or something rooted more deeply in her Islamic faith. I acknowledged the truth of an essential solitude present in our earthly life, but asked her what she would recommend to young or even older Muslims who wished to live chaste lives of sexual abstinence as they viewed marriage alone as providing the context for sexual experience and the possibility of sexual fulfilment. One couldn't deny others this fundamental human enjoyment even if it came with no guarantee of ultimate happiness or fulfilment. Sexual desire was part of being human and couldn't be repressed or denied without resulting in all kinds of other ills. Her response was that people needed to come to marriage of their own accord rather than see it as something they were expected to walk into at some stage of their young lives. She added, 'Only by living life and then seeing marriage as something which will add to your sense of contentment, should you enter into marriage; you shouldn't see marriage as a necessary prerequisite to human happiness.' Of course marriage may not guarantee anything, but I was left wondering what her advice would mean to young Muslims who wanted a healthy sexual relationship as part of an adult life but saw it as lawful and meaningful only within marriage. Muslims have traditionally understood their faith to prescribe marriage alone as the privileged space within which to engage in sexual relationships. Many will have friends of the opposite sex, but still reserve their sexual experience for marriage. How many could live their adult lives without experiencing one of the biggest blessings and pleasures of being human? While many don't wait until marriage to gain sexual experience, there is still a strong directive in most Islamic societies that sex is only permitted within marriage and that a married life is a divine blessing to be encouraged for all. As Dialmy states from his research into sexual practice:

> [The] sexual practices of Moslems often deviate from proclaimed Islamic standards, which are centred only on heterosexuality and conjugal life. These findings are exploited by Islamists; using Islam for political ends these Moslems criticise the authorities for not enforcing their co-religionists to abide by Islamic norms. Consequently, in the eyes of Islamists and, by extension, of traditionalist populations, the political leadership loses its legitimacy. For the most part Moslem populations hold traditional views on sexual norms.[32]

It seems to me that irrespective of the sexual status and practices of young Muslim men and women, we are in the danger of creating communities of deception. People are often living lives of deceit because they are ashamed, embarrassed or scared to be open about what they want. Maybe our deepest desires always remain inside of us because we struggle to relate them to our families, but a good family life is dependent on good communication. Where do young people go to be more open about their desires and aspirations, to be able to talk without being judged or reprimanded? The classical tradition outlined a way of looking at marriage which was essentially about rights and responsibilities albeit within the framework of companionship and love. But it was based on societies where puberty and sexual awareness were equated with the requirement to marry. These historically-bound traditions gave no recognition to young people who were also free and single. With the onset of modernity, financial independence and personal autonomy have allowed many people to regard marriage as a matter of personal choice rather than a family or religious obligation. Even those who are comfortable with arranged marriages often wish to have greater freedom about partner choice, and quite rightly so. It seems to me that the Islamic tradition, which recognised the power of the sexual impulse and channelled it largely into marriage, is now struggling with that other great human impulse – self-autonomy. More and more Muslim societies, while appreciating the theoretical structures of the virtuous life, are looking for meaning and self-expression in different ways. The theory of the virtuous life struggles to offer meaning to those who wish to go beyond barriers and traditional expectations, especially when it comes to the biggest decision they have to make – choosing a life partner.

THREE

Death, Dignity and the Passage of Time

I once began a public lecture with the words, 'Love and death are the two biggest stories in our lives.' Both consume our beings in different ways for, as one popular poem expresses it, 'One takes your heart, the other takes its beat.' Afterwards, a woman came up to me, smiled and said, 'Thank you for your talk, especially the opening lines. Only a woman could have begun like that.' I wasn't sure what she meant by the reference to gender but maybe men and women think and speak about love in different ways, or as Oscar Wilde said, 'I see when men love women. They give them but a little of their lives. But women when they love give everything.' It seems to me that what connects love and death is that nothing in life stirs our humanity as these two realities. If love makes death all the more poignant, death makes loving all the more essential. Dying requires us to love, be loved and then let go.

It may be that somewhere in the future as human beings we may experience another feeling, another relationship which touches our soul even more but until now wherever we look in life, the experiences of love and loving, death and dying have moved humanity more than any other human condition and reality. Many of the relationships of our youth which may have ended abruptly or angrily, even left years of bitterness, assume a different significance with age, especially when we are faced with our own mortality. Death and love give meaning, they give weight to our existence. They challenge our complacency about life, relationships and about our very existence. The difference is that most of us want love in our lives, even the all consuming kind of love, or the love which breaks our hearts, while very few would admit to waiting for death in the same way. In the late nineteenth century, Leo Tolstoy wrote about his despair in his search for the meaning of life, 'Why do I live? Why do I wish for anything, or do anything? Or expressed another way: is there any meaning in my life that will not be annihilated by the inevitability of death which awaits me?'[1]

During the course of writing this chapter, a colleague of mine, a Roman Catholic priest, passed away quite suddenly. I didn't know him that well but enough to feel shocked and sad and enough to feel a terrible heaviness throughout his funeral. Participating in funerals is encouraged in Muslim communities as such participation is regarded as an obligation which at least some Muslims must discharge on behalf of the whole community. Islamic thought mostly speaks of Muslim obligation to Muslim, but I believe that these precepts can and should be understood in the wider context of one human being to another. One doesn't need to be part of someone else's worship to feel a mutual connection to God because faith in God is not confined by religious ritual and procedures. It is about knowing that you are sharing sacred space and time with someone else who belongs to God and turns to God. Furthermore, the deceased have rights over the living, but I wasn't attending this funeral on behalf of other Muslims – I was attending because I wanted to and because witnessing death and remembering an acquaintance or a loved one is spiritually sobering.[2]

The sight of a coffin always unsettles; you know you'll see it when someone dies but you're never quite ready to accept what it means. I kept thinking of our last exchange of words only a few weeks earlier, in the corridor of our small department at the university, and the fact that I would never speak with him again. Being in a Roman Catholic church, witnessing the specific rites of the funeral and hearing the priest talk of a man 'who had given his life to God', a man who had 'lived with the tensions of being both man and priest', I couldn't help but wonder what happens to the dead who have given their lives to God in this way? I wanted to understand this particular commitment to sacerdotal chastity and this kind of struggle between the flesh and the spirit. In my mind, words like salvation and eternal kingdom didn't make sense, only that the fate of such people must be different because their struggles touch our souls. I hadn't really got to know him and all I could think of was that now I never would know him. I felt a profound sadness at this thought. As the congregation sang the beautiful and moving Catholic hymn 'On Eagle's Wings' and repeated the words 'My life is in your hands', I reflected on how we all make sense of the ultimate religious truth which I find in a stark but moving verse in the Qur'an: 'To God do we belong and to him do we return' (Q2:156). We need to remember the dead to remind ourselves of our own mortality, and it is this simple truth which can make such a difference to the way we think of ourselves, often transforming our lives. For the Muslim there is both fear and hope in this journey: the need to balance the fear of death with the joys of life. But we return to God, because we belong to God. By returning to God through death the believer will see God, meet God and this shouldn't be feared although we don't know what this seeing and meeting will be. If we see this as our primary relationship, we can live all our other earthly roles, such as as mother, sister, father, friend, in the knowledge and reassurance of this relationship. It is a relationship which reaches its culmination in death.

The first time I ever witnessed death closely was the sudden death of my mother who passed away aged 63. Prior to this I had experienced death on two other occasions: the death of an older cousin in India to whom I had grown very attached through that almost forgotten art of writing letters; and the death of my maternal grandfather. When I was told of my cousin's death, I broke down and cried because I had always felt a strong bond with him; he was one of the few people who understood me. Even though we had only met once in India, we had formed that rare kind of intellectual intimacy that survives distance and absence. I had lost a friend and this kind of loss silences you for a while. I first realised my grandfather had died when one morning I saw my mother sitting on a prayer mat in her bedroom with her hands held out. She cried softly as if remembering and mourning at the same time. She didn't say much to us; she had been his favourite child and hadn't seen him in years. Something had broken inside her, ended with his death. It never occurred to me at that age to ask my mother what a parent's death felt like and she never talked to us about it. She was a strong woman and her strength helped her always to look forward.

It was precisely because my mother was such a strong presence in our lives that it seemed inconceivable that we could continue without her. She had suffered a brain haemorrhage and was in hospital in intensive care for ten days before she passed away. It seems strange even today, 17 years later, to say 'She died' or 'She passed away', because the distressing finality of those words takes you to an unknown place. For those ten days I sat by her bed often with my younger sister, watching her lie still and just breathe, wires and tubes keeping her alive. The initial shock of seeing her like that transformed into a quiet acceptance and we consoled ourselves over cups of tea and chatter into thinking that life was welcome in whatever form; as long as her hands were warm and she breathed, we would never lose her. I was promising her things, reassuring her that all would be fine in the full certainty that my words might make a difference, that she was listening and might find her pain a little easier. Death brings to an end the possibilities of any more shared moments, only shared memories, and when you love someone, that is the most difficult thing to accept. People speak of holding onto memories to help with the grieving process, but it takes a long time for memories to offer any hope; more often memories can be crushing. Despite having two very young children, it took almost four years before I could wake up in the morning and not feel a faint ache at the front of my head reminding me that she was no longer alive. My life was full in every way, but no longer shared with her. When I saw my mother lying on the hospital bed, alongside the grief was this awesome sense of God's existence – he really does take life back. My mother was prone to sighing in the later years of her life, 'You'll see when I'm no longer here ...' or 'When I'm dead, then you'll understand ...' I never liked her speaking in this way because part of me never believed that there would come a day when she was no longer around. Her death, more than my own marriage and children, made me acutely aware of the way life moves on and things change. Although I had older brothers and sisters, none of us were prepared for the suddenness of her death; we didn't know how to console each other because we didn't know how to deal with this kind of loss. Death is universal but almost meaningless until you lose someone you love. If finding someone to love changes you, losing someone you love changes you even more – and it changed my faith and my personality. That I, too, could die at any age was a sobering thought, and when I contemplated God, I thought of death; when I prayed, I prayed to live.

The question of what happens to us beyond death has always been one of the most engaging issues for humankind and forms a key theme in world religions. We understand life when we understand death. It is important to see the two in relation to one another. Whether death is understood as part of a cyclical process in that we return as another incarnation, or a transitional moment in that we pass from one world to another, death comes as a rupture in life as we know it. Notwithstanding the medical technology which has changed the point at which we pronounce death biologically so that science seems to be constantly pushing back the time of death, by death I simply mean the end of our physical life as we experience it on this earth. Death, the grave, resurrection, the day of judgement and the afterlife are constant themes in the Qur'an; they remind us not only of earthly transience but of a final destiny with God. The relationship between this life and the afterworld lies in accepting that there is a place in time that has yet to occur; it is often depicted in terms of paradise or hell, or a garden and fire, but it is all pervasive; this other world can be imagined but it is not imaginary. Although the Qur'an repeatedly mentions a life beyond this earthly existence and events of the eschaton, the relationship between humankind, resurrection and death is a rich didactic theme in the Islamic tradition, capturing the imagination of scholars throughout history.

According to the Qur'an, death is the one event affecting all life: 'Every soul will taste death' (Q29:57), but it is also the event through which human life enters into another stage of its destiny. The end of this life is the beginning of another new life. In Islam, this transformation of earthy life is real and God-ordained. It begins in the grave but we have no definitive sense of where it ends. We may not comprehend fully what a future life after death means, but the events in an afterworld form one of the central motifs of the Qur'anic narratives, with the result that belief in the day of judgement and the afterlife became a fundamental article of faith. The afterlife and the day of judgement are explained as layers and stages of belief and this celebrated hadith is immortalised in al-Nawawi's *Forty Hadith*:

On the authority of Omar, who said: One day while we were sitting with the messenger of Allah there appeared before us a man whose clothes were exceedingly white and whose hair was exceedingly black; no signs of journeying were to be seen on him and none of us knew him. He walked up and sat down by the prophet. Resting his knees against his and placing the palms of his hands on his thighs, he said: 'O Muhammed, tell me about Islam.' The messenger of Allah said: 'Islam is to testify that there is no god but Allah and Muhammed is the messenger of Allah, to perform the prayers, to pay the zakat, to fast in Ramadhan, and to make the pilgrimage to the House if you are able to do so.' He said: 'You have spoken rightly', and we were amazed at him asking him and saying that he had spoken rightly. He said: 'Then tell me about *eman*.' He said: 'It is to believe in Allah, His angels, His books, His messengers, and the Last Day, and to believe in divine destiny, both the good and the evil thereof.' He said: 'You have spoken rightly.' He said: 'Then tell me about *ehsan*.' He said:

'It is to worship Allah as though you are seeing Him, and while you see Him not yet truly He sees you.' He said: 'Then tell me about the Hour.' He said: 'The one questioned about it knows no better than the questioner.' He said: 'Then tell me about its signs.' He said: 'That the slave-girl will give birth to her mistress and that you will see the barefooted, naked, destitute herdsman competing in constructing lofty buildings.' Then he took himself off and I stayed for a time. Then he said: 'O Omar, do you know who the questioner was?' I said: 'Allah and His messenger know best.' He said: 'He was Jebreel [Gabriel], who came to you about your religion and it was narrated by Muslim.[3]

The ethical teachings of the Qur'an are to be understood in the light of the reality of the day of judgement, for the whole of human history is a movement from creation to the eschaton. For Muslims, when this life is assessed in light of the hereafter, there is an urgency to live this life through an understanding of God's will. However, neither the time of our own death nor the day of judgement is known to us. This is one of the many secrets known only to God. Ghazali encapsulates this not knowing with not having expectations of time itself:

God's Emissary (may God bless him and grant him peace) once said to Abd Allah ibn Umar, 'In the morning-time, do not speak to yourself of the evening, and in the evening time do not speak to yourself of the morning. Take from your life something for your death, and from your health, something for your infirmity, for in truth, O Abd Allah, you do not know what your name shall be tomorrow.'[4]

The dominant Qur'anic theme regarding human destiny is that God's mercy or wrath awaits us all. A God in waiting is a constant theme in the Qur'an, a God whose promises remain.

God's compassion may mean forgiveness for every person in the end in response to an 'atom's weight of good', but we must base our lives on the constant endeavour to be morally aware, to do right and to do good deeds. This doesn't mean moral perfection but a moral struggle throughout our lives. We are responsible for our own deeds and when death comes, we are alone in death carrying into the grave and into the next life only ourselves and our actions. This was a theme expressed poignantly in Ghazali's *Letter to a Disciple*. He writes of Hatim al Assam, who said:

> I observed mankind and saw that everyone had an object of love and infatuation which he loved and with which he was infatuated. Some of what was loved accompanied him up to the sickness of death and some to the graveside. Then all went back and left him solitary and alone and not one of them entered his grave with him. So I thought and said, the best of what one loves is what will enter one's grave and be a friend to one in it. And I found it to be nothing but good deeds. So I took them as the object of my love, to be a light for me in my grave, to be a friend to me in it and not leave me alone.[5]

The relationship between good actions and faith has always been fraught with tension for those who believe in an ultimate destiny with God, and the topic has been articulated in a variety of ways. In explaining the distinctive nature of Christian faith and the doctrine of death, C. S. Lewis writes that 'The peculiarity of the Christian faith is not to teach this doctrine, but to render it, in various ways, more tolerable. Christianity teaches us that the terrible task has already in some sense been accomplished for us – that a master's hand is holding ours as we attempt to trace the difficult letters and that our script need only be a "copy"

not an original.' The great action of death has already been
communicated to humanity by Christ on Calvary.[6] In *Mere
Christianity*, Lewis continues on the significance of virtue:
that the Christian who tries to practise a life of virtue and
finds that he has failed, 'discovers his bankruptcy'. This
is because he is only giving back to God what was already
God's own. For Lewis, what the Christian God cares about is
not exactly our actions but that 'we should be creatures of
a certain kind or quality – the kind of creatures he intended
us to be – creatures related to Himself in a certain way'.[7]
Christian theology sees the purpose of God's revelation and
human actions in a particular way, as Maurice Wiles states:
'The Christian tradition has never believed that men needed
only to be shown the truth about God and about human life.
Sin has usually been regarded as more fundamental than
ignorance. Men need not only to be enlightened; they need
to be changed. The forgiveness and transformation of man
are at least as basic to Christ's mission as the impartation
of knowledge and illumination.'[8] Thus our condition of
'lostness' cannot be met by good deeds: humanity needs a
reconciliation of a radical kind.

But good deeds do matter in both Christianity and Islam
because good deeds are spiritually enriching. Jesus taught
goodness in words and in the activity of good deeds. On this
point Hannah Arendt focuses on the relevance of the private
and public in Christianity and the curious negative quality of
goodness, 'the lack of outward phenomenal manifestation'.
This is a theme which is also present in other religions, that
when goodness appears openly, it is no longer goodness even
if it is still useful as organised charity:

> Christian hostility toward the public realm, the tendency
> at least of early Christians to lead a life as far removed from

the public realm as possible, can also be understood as a self-evident consequence of devotion to good works, independent of all beliefs and expectations. For it is manifest that the moment a good work becomes known and public, it loses its specific character of goodness, of being done for nothing but goodness sake.[9]

Good deeds are significant in Islam as a reflection of good faith – not as a precursor to divine selection. Some Muslim scholars have argued that good deeds matter even though justice needs to be thought of eschatologically. Neither the righteous nor the sinner are fully requited in this life, but paradise and hell force us to contemplate the possibilities of the hereafter. For Ghazali, good deeds are intrinsic to the virtuous life, but the worshipper attains paradise – salvation – through the grace of God.

Good deeds are not only about humankind's relations with one another but with the way we have lived out our relationship with nature. A day is coming when we will all have to give an account of our stewardship over the natural world. The Jesuit scholar Thomas Michel comments in a powerfully poetic, even haunting, passage that the Qur'an invokes the day of judgement and presents the image of the natural universe rising up to accuse humankind of its crimes:

On that day, [the earth] will tell its stories, because your Lord will inspire it. On that day, humankind will come forth in small groups to show its deeds. Whoever has committed even a gram of goodness will see it then, and whoever has done even a gram of evil will see it at that time. (Q99:4-8)[10]

The concept of the earth telling her stories about man's deeds reminds us first and foremost of our accountability

to our creator. Nature has never been silent: she hears, she
sees and she feels, and in nature we find glimpses of both
humanity and divinity.

On the issue of faith and good works, Islam has often
been compared to Christianity in a less favourable light.
There is a sense that in Christianity we are bound in a
relationship with God where, as Lewis writes, the master is
'holding our hand'. In Islam, where the descent of God is
absent, there has been a tendency to equate this with divine
remoteness. On a more popular level, it is often a polemical
claim that the Christian God loves unconditionally whereas
the Muslim God turns to you only when you turn to
him, that although both faiths speak of God's love, it is
Christianity alone which speaks of God's unconditional
love. While the language of divine love is extraordinarily
powerful in the Gospels, the Christian story of divine love
is different from the Islamic story of divine mercy and
majesty. Yet, love becomes the central feature of much of
the Islamic mystical literature. There is always a certain
paradox in what we think we want and what we can actually
bear in our limited humanity when it comes to God's love,
which is his biggest mystery. There is a tradition that once
when Moses was heading towards Mount Sinai, he passed
the cave of a hermit. The hermit emerged and called after
Moses, 'Moses, ask your Lord to bestow just an atom's
weight of his divine love.' Moses agreed and talked to
God about this. God replied, 'I'll grant this servant of
mine his wish but not as much as he requested. I'll grant
him only the tiniest fraction of an atom's weight of love.'
When Moses returned from the mountain he went to see
what effect such a small amount of love would have on the
hermit. He was startled to find that instead of where the

cave had been, a part of the mountain had blown away and in its place there was a deep chasm in the earth. He cried out, 'O servant of God, what has happened? Where are you?' Then Moses looked down and saw the hermit sitting in the chasm, lost and completely overwhelmed by the love he had just experienced.

It seems that we as human beings can at best slowly journey towards God and in this journey understand over time how to be with God and how to turn to him. We may feel loved by God but we cannot endure a God revealed. The great Sufi theologian Ibn Qayyim al-Jawziyya wrote in the *Invocation of God* that the Gnostic journeys towards God on two wings, 'awareness of his own faults and recognition of his Lord's grace. He cannot journey without them, and if he denied one, he would be like a bird that had lost a wing.'[11] Thus, we journey towards God knowing that we are weak, but with hope always in his mercy. God has no need, so God does not need good deeds from us but desires good deeds as a way for us to get nearer to him rather than as a means of personal salvation. Through doing good, our hearts find true rest, and the perfect example of devotion to God is reflected in prayer. When praying, the true worshipper's heart 'is filled with awe, his head inclines and would be ashamed before his Lord to face anyone else, or to turn away'. This theme is continued:

> About these two prayers, as Hassan ibn Atiya said, 'Two men may offer prayer shoulder to shoulder, and yet between their two prayers lies a gulf as [vast] as that separating Heaven from earth. This is because one of them has his heart turned towards God while the other is forgetful and heedless. Indeed if the servant were to face a fellow man and between them lay a veil, surely there could be neither reciprocity nor intimacy. So what of the

Creator? If the servant stands before God and there is a veil of passion and whispering between him and the Lord which absorbs and fascinates his soul, and he becomes so distracted by thoughts and whispers that he is completely absent, how can there be any receptivity?[12]

What the adherents of both faiths share is the changing appreciation of scriptural language when it comes to the possible terrors of the afterlife. We are turned off by the language of fire and brimstone; the vivid images of heaven and hell, although ingrained in our cultural consciousness, seem alien. But words which speak of grace and generosity, compassion and forgiveness draw us in and slowly we begin to imagine God in a different kind of language.

It seems to me that although death and the afterlife are central themes in the Qur'an and in Islam, there is another message which weaves itself in and out of the images of heaven and hell, between this world (*dunya*) and the next world (*akhira*). It is the message of hope in divine mercy. Hope is the essence of belief and turning to God. For Ghazali, fear and hope are therapies through which the heart is cured. While both fear of God and hope in God are necessary for a virtuous life, Ghazali writes:

Hope is a commendable thing, because it is a source of incentive, and despair is reprehensible and is the antithesis of hope, because it distracts from work. Fear is not the antithesis of hope, rather it is a companion to it as its exposition will bring out ... The state of hope produces sustained spiritual combat through actions, and perseverance in obedience, however fickle circumstances might be. Among its effects are finding pleasure in unbroken acceptance with God, contentment in private prayer with Him and fondness for deferring to Him.[13]

This hope in God, this trust in God, is fundamental to our relationship with God, for without it we would live in emotional darkness, gripped by a fear of the unknown. Yet as Ghazali argues, fear is an expression of the heart's suffering but fear and hope are interdependent, in balance with each other. Still Ghazali describes hope as the higher good because hope is 'an outlet from the sea of mercy, and the outlet of fear is from the sea of wrath'.[14]

Hope and fear lie at the basis of the fundamental human condition. Man is created weak and strong, both discerning and ignorant but open to temptation, the cycle of sin followed by repentance as present in the concept of *tawba* or 'returning' to God. God for his part acting in accordance with his merciful nature will forgive. This is a continuous correlation of man–God relations. In fact, in two similar traditions, the Prophet says:

> If you had not sinned, God would have created a people who would and would have pardoned them.

> If you had not sinned, I would have feared of you what is more evil than sins. It was asked 'And what is that?' Muhammad said, 'pride.'[15]

It is the nature of this divine forgiveness which I think is the underlying message of hope in Islam. Forgiveness isn't just an act – it is a whole way of living, of conceiving the God–man relationship. Death and funerals allow the struggle with forgiveness and the possibility of human forgiveness to come to the forefront of our lives.

It is said that funerals are for the living, to give them a sense of closure, an opportunity for people to remember in their own ways what someone means to them. But I think as

we get older we all start to think how we will be remembered
by our loved ones and acquaintances. The relationship of
death to memory is a strange one because it is memory alone
which keep the dead alive. From an Islamic perspective, belief
in God requires a belief in an afterlife, belief that there is
another journey to be made. Traditional piety encourages us
to think of this world as fleeting, despite its attractions, and
the next world as the real. And yet for most of us all that we
hold precious, our desires and all that we are, belongs to this
life. We don't want even heaven to rob us of these memories.

When my mother died, my father was still alive but had
been living with a stroke for several years. I still vividly
remember the circumstances around his stroke. He had
been working away as a locum consultant in Derby when he
became ill and his colleague phoned us at home to tell us
to make our way to the hospital as soon as possible. It was
near Christmas time and he was due to come home for the
holidays. I was at home in the evening with my mother; we
were both doing what we often did in the evenings, chatting
over a cup of tea. When I put the phone down and told my
mother, we were both in such shock that for a while we
didn't know what to do or think. Yet we knew we had to go
immediately and a family friend drove us to the hospital – a
long way from where we lived. There was silence in the car,
the night seemed especially dark and when we arrived at
the hospital, we saw him looking dazed and so vulnerable.
I had never seen my father in a hospital bed because he had
never really been ill before. My mother talked to him, she
said prayers over him and she remained so strong, but I
knew that our lives had changed. However, our immediate
concerns were the practicalities of finding a place to stay
as he couldn't be moved to Huddersfield until after the

New Year. What happened next has stayed with me forever and reminds me always that the kindness of strangers is the deepest kind of kindness because it's imbued with compassion and whenever it appears, it appears as a divine gift turning despair into hope.

The consultant realised we didn't know anyone and as we asked around for a decent hotel near the hospital, he said, 'You will come and stay with me.' He was a Bengali Muslim and his offer was so genuine that my mother and I couldn't say no. We were prepared to stay in a nearby hotel but his offer spoke of something more than just shelter. Those few days we stayed with him and his wife made the sadness and difficulty of my father's situation bearable. We stayed in the hospital during the day, praying and receiving visits from family and friends, sometimes venturing out to the shops. We returned in the evening to a home-cooked meal, a table always beautifully set out and the warmth of a couple who tried to make things as normal as possible for us. I became close to them and felt that whatever happened in the future, we would always be in debt to their kindness. In the New Year my father was allowed to transfer to Huddersfield in an ambulance. There was relief, but we all wept a little as we left their home. I never saw them again.

My father's stroke and illness meant that the provider could no longer provide, the daughter was now also a carer and the parent who cared for you, now needed your care; it was sad, frustrating and humbling. My mother looked after my father, and her responsibilities and worries increased. Those of us who were at home helped her as best we could and our family home stayed our family home as long as he was alive. My father did improve, enough to smile, laugh and sit with friends, but the stroke meant he couldn't talk clearly any more. Yet he loved having visitors and continued watching the television news and glancing at the newspapers every day. Even after my mother's death, he didn't communicate much with words although he was alert to everything around him. But he had always been a man of habit and managed as long as his small comforts and needs were met. When we think of disability we often tend to discriminate about the very value of life. It is easy to talk of inherent human dignity and our moral worth, that God loves each of us equally, about our laws which should prevent against all forms of discrimination, and yet when it comes down to it, many of us feel uncomfortable around physical and mental disability. What I realised about my father was that he reconciled himself to a life with a stroke, a life that he lived with dignity and patience. Yet, despite all the love I tried to show him, I probably never quite saw him in the same way again.

When my father heard that my mother had died in the hospital he sobbed so loudly. But over the following two years I never knew how he felt the impact of her loss because he had to deal with his own disability and somehow live with surviving the death of a woman who had loved him and cared for him for so many years. So, as a family, we never fully understood what he was feeling, how much he missed her and how he now saw himself. Two people who had been married for so long, who had left their brothers and sisters back in the subcontinent, who had leant on one another to make a new life, who had sacrificed so much to build their dreams around their children – these two people, our parents, would now never again be together in the same room.

I think I found my mother's death harder because it came at a time when my own life was flourishing. I had recently begun my first lecturing position at Glasgow University, I was blessed with two beautiful healthy boys and in many ways my mother's hopes for me were all coming true. When she died there was a sense that I was no longer carrying anyone else's hopes. It was around this difficult period that I also experienced the illness of my former PhD supervisor, a person to whom I was very close and who, after my mother, probably had the biggest influence on my life. He encouraged me to broaden my reading, to understand the world of literature, of classical Islam, but perhaps most of all he helped me to know myself, to be who I wanted to be, to see the world in all its complexity and charm. On hearing of my mother's death, he sent me a card with T. S. Eliot's extract from 'Little Gidding' to remind me that my mother's death didn't mean the end of my mother's life, for the end is where we start from:

> We die with the dying;
> See, they depart, and we go with them.
> We are born with the dead:
> See, they return, and bring us with them.

He was very ill himself, suffering from pancreatic cancer, but this poem was his way of reaching out, comforting me. Even now when I think back to opening that card, reading that poem, and thinking of his death, I can still see the scratched wooden table where the small envelope lay, I can feel the card in my hand, and breaking down over the emptiness I felt inside – that memory has not faded. He died of cancer and I felt bereft. Two years later my father became ill and died in hospital. When I saw him for the last time, I remember the heaviness and guilt I felt, for I hadn't seen him much now that I had moved away. My father, this hard-working man, an exceptionally well-read man, now lay still, all his words and memories within him. I couldn't but think that although he lived in the family home with my brother's family, he had died a lonely death, having been ill and unable to express himself. As I looked at this face, so peaceful and honest, I recalled the one story which he always told with joy: that of being raised by his aunt in a small village in India. He would tell us that she treated him like a prince, that he wanted for nothing in life and yet he had travelled so far in life, in every way. We all imagine our deaths at some point in our lives: who will be near us, whose will be the last voice we hear? Yet, when death does come, it probably comes in a way we had never imagined at all. When I left that hospital, my life turned a new corner.

My memories of my parents have changed a little over time because I have learnt that one should not only remember; one has to remember rightly. The past is not always better than the present; it's just different. But the past is also a resource: it is full of failed and successful relationships, cruel and tender conversations, lost loves and hopes – and all of this is part of the present we live and the future we build. When you're young, you feel you can leave the messiness of peoples' death behind after a few years, but the death of loved ones stays with you in different ways and continues to shape your life.

My parents' deaths affected me far more than I had first imagined. It wasn't just the sense of loss and grief, but a kind of angst which meant that I was always racing against time, wanting to ensure that time didn't run out. I became scared for my own children. What if I died when they were young? Who would look after them and pass onto them all that I wanted to give them? It would not be excessive to say that while I was not paralysed by the fear of an early death, I was trapped in a certain way of thinking about loss. I wanted to do more and more with my children, as if time was running out. I would occasionally feel low at the thought of them being raised without a mother and remember one morning saying to my husband, with some relief, 'Of course, if I died you could marry again; the children would have a mother.' He looked at me in disbelief.

Thinking about death had made me more conscious of living life, of what was important. I knew I wanted things for myself and my family, but also realised that contentment in life comes with gratitude – gratitude for ordinary days and ordinary tasks. In truth I think we need to think more about death if we want to live well. It was not until my children had reached their mid-teens that there was a sense of relief – not that I had cheated death, but that I was still alive and well. I could continue to love my children, to be happy in my life, even though at the back of my mind there still lingers a strange feeling that the normality of life exists alongside the constant remembrance of death. Yet if death and conflict can mark us, they should never define us as individuals, families or communities. Whatever we experience, most of us have some choice in what we remember and how we remember. One Eid at the end of the fasting month of Ramadan, I decided to go down to West Yorkshire to celebrate the day with my brothers and sisters. It was the first time ever we had all come together with our partners and children and thus became a unique moment in our lives. As with all families, we had known our own tensions and conflicts: too much said, too little said, even years of silence between some. And yet there comes a time in all our lives when we understand that conflict should never become a permanent state. Conflict, like respect, is potent even in silence. We deny ourselves the possibilities of all kinds of happiness by not forgiving and reconciling. The Qur'an encourages forgiving others and says, 'So forgive [people's failings] with gracious forebearance' (Q15:85). Worst still, the tensions between adults plays out in the lives of their children, and another generation carries the pain without receiving any of the love. When I was growing up, my mother would often tell me to stay connected with family and relatives after her death. It was a religious and moral imperative, as the Qur'an often defined those worthy of our care and compassion to include parents, strangers, orphans and relatives. Family and relatives don't always stay together for love, but they have mutual rights and obligations to one another, especially in times of sorrow and celebration. So doing for them and being there should be seen a religious duty. Over the years, I've realised that retaining good relations really can be a challenge and yet what do we have if we don't have family friends and relatives in our lives? In the end, the visit turned out to be a good day – not because we had wiped away all the tensions, but because we all made an effort to look to the future and create new memories. I wish I had done more and said more. Life has a way of humbling us all in the end.

I believe that we can only think of death with a mixture of awe and humility even though most of us will be unprepared when it finally does come. In his analysis of spiritual growth, Scott Peck writes that death is the ultimate emptiness and that even those of us who believe in an afterlife are terrified of death. He calls dying the 'final stripping away' and that most of us fear a slow death because our 'egos can't bear the loss of dignity from watching our bodies waste away'.[16] But the physical decay of ageing is often also accompanied by situations of loneliness. Studies increasingly show that extreme loneliness on a long-term basis can be worse than obesity as a health risk, even leading to premature death.

People may be living longer but unless they feel connected to family and friends, even in retirement, the chances are that retirement or living alone becomes less about a prized independence and more about gradual isolation.

While loneliness knows no age or class barriers, its emotional and physical effects on older people makes it a potential public health issue affecting us all in the long run. In most developed countries, our increased life expectancy is a major success story of the modern age, yet as a society we are walking between two fundamental pulls in our lives – our desire for independence and personal space, and our desire to belong, whether it's among family, friends or the wider community. Human beings are relational by nature and our moral life is what happens to us in the presence of others. We need human company in our search for emotional and physical wellbeing, and while personal space – even times of solitude – may be precious to us, we can never really be happy if we feel alone. Whether it's the loneliness of unhappy relationships or simply living with no one to talk to, our desire to feel loved and remembered never leaves us.

Peck's arguments are pertinent today, as many of us are living longer lives but often with chronic illnesses. Old age holds a special kind of terror for many today, especially in societies where religion and the sense of a meaning beyond the purely material has been deprived of any worth. The apprehension held by many is that old age is the beginning of death itself. The cult of youth has made the whole process of ageing something to be feared rather than accepted as a natural part of life. In his work on death and dying, the cultural theorist Zygmunt Bauman gives a distinctive theoretical account for how we survive *death anxieties* in contemporary society and especially in Western societies.

By death anxieties Bauman means the fears and anxieties we human beings have in our awareness of our own mortality; our knowledge of our mortality is the greatest fear of all. We know that death is real but the state of death 'defies, radically and irrevocably our intellectual faculties'. Bauman follows Freud's classic theory that not only can we not imagine our own death, but that the whole process of civilisation is a self-defence mechanism to substitute for the anxieties of death. Here, culture is a collective means to 'render human mortal life bearable and even meaningful'. Yet the paradox for Freud is that it is because of this very civilisation that we suffer. For Freud, modernity may have made our lives easier but not happier and he asks 'What good is a long life to us if it is hard, joyless and so full of suffering that we can only welcome death as a deliverer?'[17]

In pre-modern societies, death was communal, with its own rights and rituals, whereas with the onset of early modern society death has become largely sequestered from public views. This view is also present in the works of the French social theorist Jean Baudrillard who claims that from the seventeenth century onwards, the 'sight of death and dying came to symbolise the abnormal in society and became institutionalised in hospitals and funeral establishments so as to be completely shunted from the public view'. Masa Higo explains that Bauman contends that through sequestration, 'the cultural force of early modern culture had removed thoughts and sights of death in order to hide any object reminiscent of mortality from the range of legitimate concerns of individuals' daily life affairs'.[18]

But if modern life has made death a sequestered event, removing it from our public consciousness, there has nevertheless been a rise in our fear of being diagnosed with a debilitating illness and losing personal dignity. Illnesses which cause premature ageing and decline make us feel that one day our lives will not be our lives any more – we will cease to be individuals in our own right but just become people other people care for. Illness can age you prematurely and so when we do think of our own death, we want to die as we have lived, just older, not sick, not dependent and most of all still with the capacity to show love and feel loved. In recent years I have spoken to several friends and colleagues who told me of their parents suffering from advanced stages of dementia. The parents live in care homes because they need specialist care. Many of them acknowledge that their parents don't even recognise them any more, and that this gradual decline can be more painful than sudden death. There is something very frightening about losing one's memory and control, because you inhabit a world where all familiarity has gradually left you, a world that has taken away your identity. Your loved ones feel helpless in trying to remind you of your past and yourself, and you feel powerless to let anyone else in.

But severe illnesses do cause loss of personal dignity and high dependency. Once, at a conference, I related my own concerns on this subject to a Jesuit scholar. I told him how recent stories in the media about assisted dying had made me even more afraid of illness as I grew older, an absolute fear of losing personal dignity as I saw it through the loss of self-autonomy. I told him that I had found myself wondering whether my religious convictions and all the ethical debates about the sanctity of human life wouldn't just crumble if I felt that my life was no longer worth living, that there was no life, only illness. I was questioning the very meaning of human dignity: is it really something we are born with or is it something we have to struggle for? In a very gentle manner he told me the story of a Christian saint who was so physically helpless in his old age and illness that he had reached the point of drifting in and out of consciousness. When he did have moments of consciousness, he would try to write something, and one of his lines was 'Now I am happy because it is only now that I am completely in God's hands.' I was silenced and felt slightly ashamed of myself because of the strength of this faith, the absolute surrender of the self with such a deep belief in God's love. There are similar stories across religions, especially in the more mystical genres of literature, but sometimes you need to hear another religious voice to understand the issue you're struggling with, to look deeper into your own faith in order to find the resources to sustain you and even challenge your vulnerabilities.

The concept of human dignity is used in all kinds of ways nowadays, often as a short cut to talk about human rights. But human dignity as it has been traditionally understood in religions is struggling to persuade people of the inherent sanctity of human life. The boundaries between intrinsic and extrinsic dignity are gradually being blurred as societies differ on what it means to be human. The focus on humanity lies both in the biological make-up of humankind and its inherent distinction in relation to the rest of God's physical and natural creation. This distinction has been expressed in terms of dignity and nobility, for example the Islamic tradition's claims that human beings are created in the best of forms (*fi ahsani taqwim*) and are also the noblest of creation (*ashraf al-makhluqat*). But this dignity is a complex term, tying man to God and nature in physical and metaphysical ways. Human dignity in general has been a widely used term in religious scholarship, with significant implications for human life, and yet the concept is open to a variety of meanings. The word dignity, rooted in the Latin *dignus* and *dignitas*, both meaning 'worthy of esteem or honour', has come down to us from the classical tradition. But in both Greek and Roman thought, the concept of universal human dignity did not exist; the concept was applicable to human beings, but not *all* human beings. The Romans identified the person of *arête*, virtue or excellence, as one who could merit dignity. The Stoics leaned towards a more humanitarian brotherhood of all and claimed that since all human beings had reason, they could all have an intrinsic dignity if they lived a life which was essentially rational, self-reflective and in accordance with their natural surroundings. But intrinsic human worth could not be universally applied in the Greek world since inequality was a natural feature of life. The emphasis on distinction and hierarchy within humanity in much of Greek philosophy meant that dignity, implying honour and esteem, was not viewed as an inalienable characteristic of all mankind, rather something which only a few possessed: human value was acquired rather than inherent.

Christian theology is generally rooted in the fundamental concept that human dignity should be viewed as universally applicable. The concept of *imago Dei*, 'man made in the image of God' (Genesis 1:26–27), has been a central, though not singular, concept for elaborating the relationship between man and God. However this likeness is to be understood, the phrase signifies that human beings are created by God purposefully, not just as his creatures but creatures who themselves are godlike in some way. But beyond this, as Hannah Arendt argues, the Christian emphasis on the sacredness of life was also accompanied by the belief that what matters is not immortality but that life is the highest good:

The modern age continued to operate under the assumption that life, and not the world, is the highest good of man; in its boldest and most radical revisions and criticisms of traditional beliefs and concepts, it never even thought of challenging this fundamental reversal which Christianity had brought into the dying ancient world. No matter how articulate and how conscious the thinkers of modernity were in their attacks on tradition, the priority of life over everything else had acquired for them the status of a 'self-evident truth.'[19]

What is fundamental to a religious understanding of human life is that humanity has been created for a purpose in this life notwithstanding the promise of the life to come. In Islam, the Qur'anic account of man's creation is simultaneously also an account of man's vocation in life:

> Behold, thy Lord said to the angels, 'I will create a vicegerent on earth.' They said, 'Wilt thou place therein one who will make mischief and shed blood while we do sing thy praises and glorify thy holy name?' He said, 'I know what ye know not.' And he taught Adam the names of all things. (Q2:30)

> Behold, thy Lord said to the angels, 'I am going to create man from clay. When I have finished him and breathed into him of my spirit, fall down in obedience to him.' (Q38:71–72)

Adam's being was complete only with divine breath, but it is difficult to understand what this breath means for human beings from birth to death. The anthropomorphic image of a God blowing into a theomorphic human frame remains powerful but mysterious. At the time that Adam was a mere form, body without spirit, it is said that the angels marvelled at Adam's strange form and figure, for they had never seen anything like it before. Indeed Iblis himself looked at it for a long time before saying, 'God has created this thing for some great purpose. Perhaps he himself has gone inside it.' It is in the *Tales of the Prophets* that we have the description of the breath gradually permeating all of Adam:

> They will ask you concerning the spirit. Answer, the spirit was created at the command of my Lord (Q17:85). God ordered the spirit to be immersed in all the lights then he commanded it to enter Adam's body with praise and without haste. The spirit seeing a narrow entrance and narrow apertures said, 'Oh Lord how can I enter?' It was told to enter reluctantly and exit reluctantly.[20]

Human dignity remains one of the most difficult states to define. In some way it is like justice, in that we can all recognise when it's being violated but we can't quite define what it is. In his novel, *The Pilgrimage*, Paulo Coelho describes dignity in the human effort to live meaningfully while aware of the reality of death:

> Human beings are the only ones in nature who are aware that they will die. For that reason and only for that reason, I have a profound respect for the human race, and I believe that its future is going to be much better than its present. Even knowing that their days are numbered and that everything will end when they least expect it, people make of their lives a battle that is worthy of a being with eternal life. What people regard as vanity-leaving great works, having children, acting in such a way as to prevent one's name from being forgotten – I regard as the highest expression of human dignity.[21]

But human dignity sits alongside that most fundamental predicament, human restlessness. Poets and writers have wrestled with the question of human restlessness: why do we feel that we are always searching, looking for a beauty for some meaning, for some contentment in ourselves, in our relationships and often in something beyond ourselves which we can't quite define? Maybe this restlessness is the cause of this breath in that something of the divine within us make us long to return to the divine, as St Augustine reflected, 'You have made us for yourself O Lord and our heart is restless until it rests in you.' Our restlessness may actually be a desire for peace, for some stillness in our lives. Yet restlessness can be what makes us more noble creatures, or as Pascal says:

> Nothing is so insufferable to man as to be completely at rest, without passions, without business, without diversion, without study. He then feels his nothingness, his forlornness, his insufficiency, his dependence, his weakness, his emptiness. There will immediately arise from the depth of his heart weariness, gloom, sadness, fretfulness, vexation, despair.[22]

If this breath is the reason why human beings are moral agents, able to reason and conceptualise, to think of life beyond simply survival on this earth, then human dignity lies in this consciousness, this awareness that our existence has purpose and meaning. The philosopher and poet Allama Iqbal equated the primordial story of the Fall with this consciousness when he wrote that the purpose of the Qur'anic legend of the Fall is that the 'Fall does not mean moral depravity; it is man's transition from simple consciousness to the first flash of self consciousness, a kind of waking from the dream of nature with a throb of personal causality in one's own being'.[23] To be human is to seek that knowledge which enhances our awareness of our self and provides an insight to what makes us human.

But if human dignity, the sanctity of human life, has been framed largely in religious terms, today the increased emphasis on transparency in institutions, including religious institutions, reveals a disturbing reality. The sexual and psychological abuse of children and adults across religious organisations, but particularly within the Roman Catholic Church, highlights the suffering and humiliation of ordinary people, people who placed their trust in the very organisations which developed the concept of dignity as the defining essence of our humanity. These institutions, which upheld the concept of dignity for centuries, have in many cases failed the very people they were meant to serve and protect.[24] They have done so by remaining silent.

Economic principles are also in play, so that we are always evaluating consciously or subconsciously the life of the individual. In his political philosophy, Michael Sandel explores how we are drifting from having a market economy to being a market society. The question he poses is whether we want a society where everything is up for sale? He states that 'a market economy is a tool – a valuable and effective tool – for organizing productive activity. A market society is a way of life in which market values seep into every aspect of human endeavour. It's a place where social relations are made over in the image of the market.'[25] For Sandel, morality and spiritual concerns about the common good have been crowded out by free market ethics but he argues that this recent phenomenon of money being able to buy almost anything is neither good for democracy nor human welfare. In most recent times, during an age of economic recession and austerity, the argument that human beings have an intrinsic worth, beyond their economic value to the state, has also come to the fore. In an astute and moving piece, the left-wing columnist and feminist Laurie Penny writes that we are not telling young people – those who are struggling to cope – the truth in order to save them from despair:

> However worthless you feel, you deserve to have enough to eat, somewhere to live, clothes on your back and other vital parts, to be loved, to know that you matter. You deserve those things whatever is happening with the economy, because everyone does, because human beings are worth more than their usefulness to capital. The most important political battles are fought on the territory of imagination.[26]

One of the most eloquent expressions of humankind's ability to live, seek and be moved by the suffering and indignity of others is encapsulated in the memorable lines of the philosopher Bertrand Russell:

> Three passions, simple but overwhelmingly strong, have governed my life: the longing for love, the search for knowledge, and unbearable pity for the suffering of mankind ... Love and knowledge, so far as they were possible, led upward toward the heavens. But always pity brought me back to earth. Echoes of cries of pain reverberate in my heart. Children in famine, victims tortured by oppressors, helpless old people a hated burden to their sons, and the whole world of loneliness, poverty and pain make a mockery of what human life should be. I long to alleviate this evil, but I cannot, and I too suffer.[27]

It is our consciousness, free will and the autonomy to make moral choices which separates us from the rest of creation, but dignity remains a vague concept even though its essence may be linked with a transcendental being and to a transcendental status. Here, I would argue that while human organ donation and transplantation have become far more widespread in the last ten years or so, the related issues touch on many of our deepest concerns around life and death. For some, it may seem misguided if not morally reprehensible that all of society is not prepared to ameliorate the suffering of others. But others fear that the increased pressure to donate organs risks devaluing human life itself, by treating the human body as a commodity which loses its use, indeed its value, after death. Most religions believe in the intrinsic sanctity of the human being and the human body even after death. The dead are not some public resource to be used for the welfare of the living. The dead point to the afterlife, the possibility of another world and the hope of a new life. So organ donation is often seen as a violation of the human body as it enters the mystery of an afterlife. But if we are to judge human progress through medical advancement and its objective of healing the sick on this earth, we have to sever this link. Donation is not an obligation but a gift. It needs to be regarded as a moral good in itself where, despite the physical intrusion, the deceased remains spiritually untouched. Medicine is increasingly trying to pull human beings away from the edge of death so that life continues. But life continues for many people in a desperate and wretched physical and psychological state in which there is no longer any sense of self-dignity. Indeed the philosopher and ethicist Ruth Macklin comments that human dignity is not only a vague concept but adds nothing to the topic of bioethical issues even if some consider dignity as a transcendental ideal.[28] Indeed the word 'dignity' lacks any settled interpretation and has been regarded by some as redundant to the concerns around human life and bioethics. However, Peck distinguishes between the two kinds of human dignity: a true dignity and a false dignity; true dignity equated with the soul, and false dignity equated with the ego. Peck argues that if we think of dignity as ego then our egos 'can't bear the loss of dignity from watching our bodies waste away'. The ego tries to rebel when in reality it faces a losing battle. However, the soul 'welcomes the stripping away process. We can learn that as we give up control we are also giving up false dignity.'[29] It is, however, hard to feel comforted by this kind of exposition even though many will agree with Peck that fundamentally faith in God demands this kind of letting go. It is hard because people of faith live in the belief that our ultimate destiny is with God, yet most of us do not wish to think of death and the gradual demise of our bodies. As Pascal says, 'As men are not able to fight against death, misery, ignorance, they have taken it into their heads, in order to be happy, not to think of them at all.'[30]

How we imagine God is how we imagine our destinies. Despite understanding God as the transcendent Other, Islamic thought has from the earliest times wrestled with how divine presence manifests itself in this world and how humans can understand themselves as God's agents of the 'divine breath'. Though Adam's descent on earth is regarded as a new paradigm for human existence, it seems that something between the human and the divine has been ruptured in this exile and that the longing for a return retains a powerful hold. Mankind is thus intrinsically theomorphic. In Ghazali's *Letter to a Disciple*, the author cautions, 'O disciple live as long as you want, but you must die, love whatever you want, but you will become separated from it, and do what you want but you will be repaid for it.'[31] Some, however, have stressed that for the faithful, death is the seamless entry from one life to another, where worship and prayer is not interrupted. The founder of the great Sufi Qadiriya order, Abd al-Qadir al-Jilani, said, 'Our Master the Prophet describing the state of the believer who achieves truth through remembrance, says "Believers do not die. They only pass from this temporal life to the everlasting life." And they do there what they did here. As he says, "The prophets and the ones close to Allah continue their worship in their graves as they did in their houses." The worship he mentions is inward supplication of Allah, not the prayer obligatory five times a day in this world, with its standing, bowing and prostration. Inward supplication is one of the principal qualities identifying the true believer.'[32]

However temporal this life may be, it is the only life we know and most of us fear its end even if this means a new beginning. Some of the most poignant accounts of death lie in people's fear of death. Jorge Luis Borges speaks of death as making men 'precious and pathetic' where our 'phantom condition' makes humankind moving since every act may be our last. In his short story *The God's Script*, Borges describes a prisoner's feeling of gradual obliteration as he lies terrified on the prison floor. The prisoner has a series of broken dreams where the prison is filling up with grains of sand which will ultimately suffocate him. He writes, relieved to be alive, 'A man becomes confused, gradually, with the form of his destiny; a man is, by and large, his circumstances. More than a decipherer or an avenger, more than a priest of the god, I was one imprisoned. From the tireless labyrinth of dreams I returned as if to my home to the harsh prison. I blessed its dampness, I blessed its tiger, I blessed the crevice of light, I blessed my old suffering body, I blessed the darkness and the stone.'[33] Yet it is Borges who reminds us of the human desire for immortality, in which monotheism emphasises the next world while clinging on to this life:

> To be immortal is commonplace; except for man, all creatures are
> immortal; for they are ignorant of death; what is divine, terrible,
> incomprehensible, is to know that one is immortal. I have noted
> that, in spite of religion, this conviction is very rare. Israelites,
> Christians and Moslems profess immortality, but the veneration
> they render this world proves they believe only in it, since they
> destine all other worlds, in infinite number, to be its reward or
> punishment.[34]

I think that if my parents were still alive today, I wouldn't
think of death so much; it would still seem far away in the
future. Yet, their absence makes death present, and much of
my own adult life has been spent thinking about the world
in which I live now against the background of their death. In
a way, life has become complex, more meaningful and more
productive. Your parents' death removes a certain gaze on
your life, a protective gaze. Yet once they were no longer alive
I realised that I didn't need them for security but I missed
them as people I loved. You learn to live and love in new
ways and you learn to face your challenges in new ways. Then
there is always the hope that the concept of *sadaqa jariya* – a
continuous charity – lives through you and reflects on them.
According to the Islamic tradition,

> If a human dies, then his good deeds stop except for three: a *sadaqa
> jariah* [continuous charity], a beneficial knowledge, or a righteous
> child who prays for him.[35]

Other people's death affects me in new ways. I think about
their lives in a way that I hadn't when I was younger. Many
years ago a family friend died quite suddenly. He was a
Muslim, and in accordance with Islamic tradition the funeral
had to take place quite quickly. However, the family informed
us that he had wished to be buried in India and that they

would be flying his body back to the small Indian village where his parents lay buried. A vigorous discussion broke out as to whether this was the right thing to do and whether his friends and relatives in the UK could pay their respects if he was to be flown thousands of miles away. The funeral would be delayed, goodbyes left unsaid and those nearest might never get closure. But since then I have learnt that there are many ways to pay respect and to remember, not just those we knew but those we never knew. As the years go by, I think that if I am lucky I will be able to understand the theologies of death, although the beauty and sensuality of the afterlife as depicted in Qur'an is not what I think of when I think of death. There is a disconnect between scripture and sentiment here because the afterlife fails to appease the anxiety surrounding death. Many of us think of the afterlife in terms of a new creation, or a heaven, a place where we will be reunited with family and friends who have died. Yet the traditions depicting the afterlife also say that it is only in the next life that we will be able to witness God: 'On that day, some faces will be radiant, looking at their Lord' (Q75:22–23). I wonder whether any of us can imagine what it will be like to be with God?

FOUR

Christians, Muslims and Dialogue

When I was growing up, conversations about Christians or Christianity were very rare. My friends never talked about religion or faith, and so at school my only understanding of Christianity was through the experiences of Christmas and to some extent Easter. We had never been inside a church nor did I understand worship of any kind outside my own faith. When it came to family discussions about religion, I only have vague memories of my mother occasionally referring to Christians in the Qur'an and the big theological divide between Christianity and Islam which was always centred on the person of Jesus and the Christian views of his divinity. I don't remember ever being interested or intrigued by any particular religious discourse. I was always a Muslim to my friends, but in my mind my friends weren't Christian – they were just British. That was how they wanted to be seen and that was how they described themselves. We talked of different religions in Religious Education classes but I don't remember my friends talking of religious faith or whether they were practising Christians in any meaningful way. The only time in my childhood that I was truly conscious and drawn to the sacred reality of Christianity was through music, when I listened to hymns in assemblies, choral music and Christmas carols. I found many of the Christmas carols moving, uplifting and simply beautiful. The music, the words and the voices made me feel connected to God in a markedly different way; they drew me in and I found myself relating emotionally to another way of praising God.

Later in my life, my doctoral studies focused on Islamic jurisprudence and thus again Christian theology did not really enter my consciousness for many years. My supervisor was raised a Roman Catholic but I always understood him to be an agnostic and we never discussed Christianity. My interest in Christian–Muslim relations came about really by chance and developed gradually when I became a university lecturer. However, I have now been actively engaged in reflecting on the dialogue between Christianity and Islam for many years. By 'engagement' I mean sitting down with Christian and Muslim scholars in various places around the world to reflect on the theology and history of these two global religions. The consequence of this engagement has drawn me to the way Christians talk of God and inspired within me a much deeper interest in the theological themes and conversations between the world's two largest faiths. Furthermore, the encounters I had, the friendships I made throughout this engagement, have prompted a desire to know more deeply about the Christian faith and how faith speaks to faith in ever changing socio-political landscapes.

Dialogue itself is a contested term, being neither a defined nor a systematic discipline. It has, however, been an intellectual and ethical imperative for many scholars and practitioners of religion over the last few decades. Its rationale is that even if the concept is ill-defined, the word has become an umbrella term for any kind of multi-faith activity which brings people of different faiths and cultures together; it is essentially about communicating for and towards a more peaceful coexistence. The social dimension of dialogue has also seen the growth of the value and importance of theological openness to other religious traditions. This has involved, amongst other things, exploring religious difference and the complex concepts of the 'Other' and 'Religious Otherness' as featured in the writings and legacy of Emmanuel Levinas. Levinas's critique of the Western philosophical tradition was that it lacked the ability to account for the Other *as* other. If religious traditions are to engage in mutual understanding, then the fundamental basis of this exercise has to be mutual respect not projection of oneself or one's own religious prejudices.

Much of dialogue tries not to let the inner diversity of any one religion get in the way of faith speaking to faith. Thus, race, background, sectarian differences and issues of politics and economics are ignored by the participants. Many claim that this is a fundamental weakness of dialogue, as it reduces the inner complexities of the faiths and the participants who wish to remain individuals rather than simply be defined as practitioners of a faith. Dialogue and reconciliation often go hand in hand, as both have risen largely from the vestiges of a post-colonial Christian world. Both words also link to the fact that interpersonal relationships contribute effectively to the creation of sustainable human relations, and this is an absolute imperative if we are to create peaceful and more compassionate societies.

People's engagement in various forms of dialogue, whether in universities, churches or socially in their communities, has grown over the last two decades. The willingness to listen to others, to learn about another faith, is increasingly viewed as a moral good even if it is difficult to quantify what this kind of activity achieves within communities. One reason for the rise in intellectual curiosity is the fundamental changes in our attitude to conceptualising and defining the meaning of truth. Our understanding of truth and grasp of reality has been undergoing a radical shift over the decades. More and more of us appreciate the philosophical and sociological problems in talking of truth in absolutist terms. We recognise the difficulties of speaking of one truth even if we believe in the truth of our own religion or perspective. We also recognise the limits of language in how we talk of truth and transcendence. Most importantly, most of us who value dialogue in a variety of forms know that absolutist views of truth are not conducive to mutual learning and the spirit of self-reflection, which are necessary ingredients of a moral life and a life of learning. This is not some soft liberalism or a call to relativise everything, but actually a call for humility. Whatever our personal convictions, human beings only learn when they engage with others to open up new ways of thinking about the things which really matter in life. This is how we grow and eventually open ourselves to receiving and challenging traditional wisdom.

The idea of religious community, representation and leadership also makes it important to reflect on who represents whom in dialogue settings. Religions have varying views on the nature and purpose of religious authority and also the visual representation of religious authority in institutional and public life. This has naturally raised concerns over gender, namely the relative lack of women's voices and how women are so often the consumers of religion whereas men are the producers of religion. To quote Joseph Conrad, 'God is for men and religion is for women.'

1. Mona Siddiqui in her family home with her sons Suhaib, Zuhayr, and Fayz and husband Farhaj, 2011.

2. Mona in Karachi at the age of 4 with her family, her grandparents and some of her uncles, aunts and cousins.

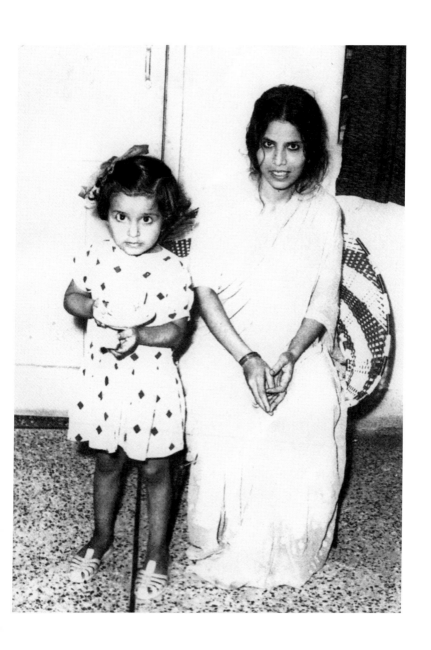

3. Mona's passion for tea began early as she sips morning tea in her Karachi home with her mum.

4. Mona with her parents and older sister, Khadijah, a few months before they left Karachi for England.

5. A family picnic near Glasgow in 1996
with Mona's eldest son, Suhaib, happily
eating fried chicken!

6. Mona's first visit to Karachi with her own children in December 2007. The family attended her cousin's wedding and her younger brother Ashar went with them.

7. Mona's honorary doctorate from the
University of Huddersfield in 2009. A
proud moment as she returned with her
family to the town where she grew up.

8. Mona with her OBE in 2011, for services to inter-faith relations.

Christian–Muslim theological dialogue has also been a rather gendered discipline. In almost all of the meetings, seminars and conferences I have attended over these past years, there have always been more men than women in attendance and participating as speakers. On the Islamic side, it has to be said, I have met very few women participants, especially those who would claim to have any real interest in or knowledge of Christian thought, even if they have a rigorous interest and experience of the varying concepts of dialogue. There are all kinds of historical and intellectual reasons for this, but I regard the academic world of dialogue as a largely male-dominated field in which we need more female voices. I have personally stayed engaged because I believe academics have an obligation to wider society, and influencing public thinking is in my view an ethical imperative. It is also unfortunate that many academics become so obsessed with keeping their disciplines distinct that they see no merit in engaging in dialogue across religious traditions. But they often fail to see that what really matters is that all our academic disciplines can have a life beyond books and articles. I strongly believe that the purpose of all learning should be about changing oneself and thereby the world in some small way. The academy can be an end in itself, but we also have a moral imperative to engage with public life if we feel that the interaction can make even the smallest contribution to human and societal moral progress. We are all in the present and all share the future.

There are many ways to look at the history of Christian–Muslim engagement throughout the centuries. Both these religions have complex histories involving schisms, conflicts and coexistence. These events shaped theological and philosophical perspectives which continue to influence mutual perceptions and understandings. The schisms in Christianity became manifest mainly through the Eastern Orthodox, Roman Catholic and Protestant traditions; and in Islam principally through the Sunni–Shi'a sectarian divide, although many other groups followed this split. These divisions remain and continue to find new ways of emerging as theological and political conflicts. Outside institutional structures, various kinds of mystical dimensions retained their distinct approach to the search for God. In Islam, Sufism developed within orthodoxy yet created particular ways of reflecting on God and following the desire to be near to God.[1]

While many people engaged in dialogue today are not particularly concerned with doctrinal differences, part of theological and thus ethical dialogue is to explore what people believe and how this then affects the way they relate to others. This is not a mere exercise of the present; it has a history during which great minds formulated views about other people's faiths through the prism of their own faith. Thus, I think it is necessary to return to what was actually said by major thinkers on both sides because doctrine has always been important to both religions, even if very few people today talk of doctrinal differences.

Islam came after Christianity and spread in Christian lands. So in many ways Islam's response to Christianity came after its own reception by the Christian world, which responded to this new religion with curiosity as well as hostility:

> The rapid rise of Islam in the seventh and eight centuries placed Christian thinkers in an unaccustomed position. From its earliest days Christianity had defined itself against classical paganism on the one hand and Judaism on the other, but the religion of

Muḥammad demanded a different response, for it proclaimed itself the very culmination of Christianity.[2]

Politics and theology were intertwined in the Christian assessment of Islam. Eirenic as well as hostile attitudes to Islam among the Christians of the East reflected the positive aspect of Islam (from a Christian perspective), which was the affirmation of one God, and its negative doctrine that denied the divinity and meaning of Christ in Christian life and devotion. Many of the Christian writers of the East placed Islam in the broad context of a monotheistic belief but critiqued the religion for its misunderstanding or denial of Christ's salvific status. The source of all the controversy around Jesus in Islam is to be found in the Qur'an itself. One of the modern Muslim thinkers who has written on Christianity, Hasan Askari, states that 'Islam is the only religion outside Christianity where Jesus is again really present. In other religions, Jesus is not part of their sacred scriptures.'[3] Askari is right to the extent that Jesus is present in the Qur'an in a way that contrasts with any other religious faith. But Jesus is not central to Islam's understanding of God in the same way as he is in the Christian faith. This non-centrality but acceptance of Jesus as a prophet with the epithet, *ruh Allah*, or 'spirit of God', has often created a rather peculiar theological tension between the two faiths. Nevertheless, Muslim reflections on the life and ministry of Jesus is not monolithic and has led to Jesus being understood in a variety of ways in the various Islamic intellectual and literary disciplines. A brief glimpse at certain Qur'anic verses shows us this complexity:

Those who believe and those who are Jewish and Christians and who believe in Allah and the last day and work righteousness, shall have their reward with the Lord, and on them will be neither fear nor will they grieve. (Q2:62)

Christ Jesus, the son of Mary, was no more than messenger of Allah and his word which he bestowed on Mary and a spirit proceeding from him. Say not three; it will be better for you Allah is one God. (Q4:171)

O People of the Book, do not exaggerate in your religion nor utter anything concerning Allah save the truth. The Messiah, Jesus, son of Mary, was only a messenger of Allah and His word which he cast upon Mary and a spirit form Him ... Do not say 'three' – cease! it is better for you. Allah is only one God. Far is it removed from His transcendent majesty that he should have a son. (Q4:171)

Jesus said, 'Indeed, I am the servant of Allah. He has given me the Scripture and made me a prophet. He has made me blessed wheresoever I be; and He has enjoined on me prayer and charity as long as I live. He has made me kind to my mother, and not overbearing or miserable. So peace is on me the day I was born, the day that I die, and the day that I shall be raised up to life [again]!' Such was Jesus the son of Mary. It is a statement of truth, about which they [vainly] dispute. It is not befitting to [the majesty of] God that He should beget a son. Glory be to Him! When He determines a matter, He only says to it, 'Be,' and it is. (Q19:30–35).

That they said [in their boast], 'We killed Christ Jesus The son of Mary, The Messenger of Allah' – but they killed him not, nor crucified him, but so it was made to appear to them, and those who differ therein are full of doubts, with no [certain] knowledge, but only conjecture to follow, for of a surety They killed him not – Nay, Allah raised him up unto Himself; and Allah is Exalted in Power and Wise. (Q4:157–158)

Even a cursory examination of these Qur'anic verses reveals that the Qur'anic Jesus is viewed in a fundamentally different light from the Jesus of Christian faith. Jesus' divinity is central to any Christian Christology, and any religion or new ideology that did not recognise this had to be essentially false, even if attempts were made to understand it. The Qur'anic story of Jesus is about Jesus the prophet, not Jesus the Messiah. This emphasis on prophecy also points to two different discourses between Muslims and Christians. Islam does not have Christology central to its doctrine of God, but it does have a Christology of sorts because the Qur'an speaks of Jesus in multiple ways. Christian doctrine, Christians (*nasara*) and Muslim attitudes to them as communities of believers is alluded to over a hundred times in the Qur'an. Jesus, or Isa as he is called in the Qur'an, is mentioned in 15 *suras* of the Qur'an and in 93 verses as either 'sign', 'mercy' or 'example'. Jesus is a revered prophet in the whole historical chain of prophets and the argument, according to Muslim theology, is that he never claimed to be anything else but a servant of God; thus he was similar to all the other prophets. Yet in the Qur'an, Jesus is also the Prophet, Word and Messenger of God. Even though there is no one particular Jesus narrative which brings together the Christic, miraculous and prophetic nature of Jesus under his most dramatic epithet, 'spirit of God' (*ruh Allah*), this epithet defines Jesus as one chosen by God in both Islamic and Christian belief.

While prophecy as a conceptual paradigm of God's purpose remained central to Islam, it gradually assumed a lesser relevance in Christianity. Here, in the person of Jesus, God himself was present and thus the status of prophecy was eclipsed by the doctrine of the Incarnation. The divine/human nature of Christ unfolded as a unique event which went far beyond prophetic mission and guidance for Christians. For Muslims, however, this Christic complexity was for the most part refuted in the emphasis on God's oneness and the essence of his transcendental otherness. The central theological divide between Islam and Christianity remains the person and essence of Jesus, and for this reason alone, many Muslims and Christians remain convinced that dialogue between the two religions, however understood, is fundamentally flawed. Islam came after Christianity, and while the Qur'an affirms the faith, Islamic belief ultimately rejects the very essence of the Christian faith: the divinity of Christ and thus the descent of God.

It was against this background that early Christian writers tried to understand Islam but also critique it for its ignorance of the truth of Christianity. Islamic monotheism was welcome but most Christians writing about Islam saw this as a powerful threat to Christian lands. One of the first people to engage with Islam and its doctrinal heresies was John of Damascus, a Christian monk and priest of the eighth century and one of the last fathers of the Eastern Orthodox Church. He is known for his defence of icons, as John's own context was one where internal doctrinal divisions between various Christian groups meant that he was writing for other Christians as well as against the new religion of Islam. However understood or misunderstood Islam was, most Christians who learnt of Islam recognised that the oneness of God formed the very basis of Muslim monotheism. But if unity in the Trinity was the most confusing aspect of Christian doctrine for Muslims, the Qur'anic message of divine unity was derided because Muhammad's claims about prophecy and scripture were deemed to be false. John, too, scoffed at the Muslim belief in the divine origins of the Qur'an, accusing Muhammad of falsely claiming that 'scripture had been brought down to him from heaven' whereas in fact the Qur'an's pronouncements were worthy of scorn.[4] But if John empathised with Muslim monotheism, he was also well aware that Muslims saw Christian monotheism in a very different light. He was not prepared to accept the Muslim accusation that Christians were themselves actually 'Associators' (*mushrikin*) because they saw Christ as the 'Son of God'. In a fierce theological attack, he writes:

> The Muslims accuse the Christians of being 'Associators' for ascribing a partner to God, by calling Christ 'son of God', and 'God.' The Christians in turn accuse the Muslims of being 'Mutilators', by having disassociated God from His word and Spirit.[5]

For John, if Christ is a Word and a Spirit coming from God, he must be in God and thus he must be God. When Muslims deny this they separate and place outside of God what is part of God, thus mutilating God. If one takes Word and Spirit away from God, then God becomes an inanimate object like a stone or a piece of wood. For John, the Muslim God was therefore lifeless. I quote John of Damascus as one of the earliest examples of a Christian polemic, although it seems to me that despite some variations the doctrinal discussions between Christians and Muslims has stayed on the same course throughout the centuries. During the sixteenth century, Martin Luther, who saw both the challenge and the lure of the Turks and Islam for his fellow Christians, wrote a critique of Muslim doctrine. In Luther's view, Islam was fundamentally a divine punishment for Christians for their sins. He admired the piety of Muslims and praised much in Islamic culture, yet his critique of Muslim doctrine was based on the bedrock of his theology – the incarnation of God in Christ. Luther wrote that it was Christological doctrines which distinguished Christianity 'from all other faiths on earth'. Muslims did not recognise or accept this and thus Muhammad, claimed Luther, was 'a destroyer of our Lord Christ and his kingdom'.[6] Without recognising the divinity and redemptive work of Christ, 'all Christian doctrine and life are gone'. Muslim refutation of Jesus' sonship was ridiculed because Luther saw Islam as a religion preoccupied with the flesh. Thus he retorted:

> Christians know full well how God can have a son and it is not necessary that Muḥammad teach us how God must first become a man and have a woman to produce a son or a bull must have a cow to produce a calf. Oh how overpowered in the flesh of women Muḥammad is. In all his thoughts, words and deeds, he cannot speak nor do anything apart from this lust. It must always be flesh, flesh, flesh.[7]

Even when we come to the early part of the twentieth century, the American missionary Samuel Zwemer (1867–1952) felt that the need to evangelise amongst Muslims was paramount. He viewed 'the dead weight of formality called tradition' as 'Islam's intolerable burden'.[8] It was this tradition which had gradually led to the demise of Islam's glory and political power and yet a gap had been created as a result of this demise. Zwemer saw this as an opportunity for 'a divine preparation for the evangelization of Moslem lands and the winning of Moslem hearts to a new allegiance. Jesus Christ is sufficient for them as He is for us.'[9] Yet Zwemer saw that Christ's life had no devotional presence in the piety of Muslims. For Muslims, Muhammad was the prophet par excellence, the one chosen by God. Zwemer understood the global phenomenon that was and is Islam, but again expressed his sadness over the absence of Jesus in the life of the Muslim:

> As in a total eclipse of the sun the glory and the beauty of the heavenly orb are hidden, and only the corona appears on the edge, so in the life and thought of Mohammedans their own Prophet has almost eclipsed Jesus Christ. Whatever place He may occupy in the Koran – and the portrait there given is a sad caricature; whatever favourable critics may say about Christ's honourable place among the Moslem prophets, it is nevertheless true that the large bulk of Mohammedans know extremely little and think still less, about Jesus Christ. He has no place in their hearts nor in their lives.[10]

Muslims, for their part, from the beginning accused Christians of distorting the original message of Jesus. On the charge of distortion or corruption (*tahrif*), Sidney Griffith writes:

> From the early Islamic period onward, the charge and countercharge of corrupting the scriptures became a staple in arguments about religion between Jews, Christians and Muslims. On the one hand, Muslim writers were concerned to claim the authority of the Bible to warrant the scriptural authenticity of Muhammad, the Qur'an and Islamic teaching more generally; one may call this process the 'Biblicizing' of the Islamic prophetic claims. On the other hand given the concomitant Islamic contention that the earlier scriptures were corrupt and therefore of questionable authenticity, along with the divergent cast of many Islamic presentations of Biblical narratives, one might also speak of a simultaneous process of 'Islamicizing' the biblical material.[11]

Against this general background of doctrinal and scriptural charges and countercharges, little attempt was made to understand the Christian explanations of monotheism which emphasised the plurality of natures in God, not three separate entities in the Godhead. Nor did Muslims pay much attention to what Christ meant in Christian devotion. An example of this lies in the works of the tenth-century theologian and jurist al-Baqillani. In the following extract, al-Baqillani asks about the Trinity, where the Son and the Holy Spirit are particularities of the Father. His point is that if all three hypostases are equal then why could the Father not be a particularity of the Son and Holy Spirit?

> Say to them: If the hypostases are one substance, and the Father's substance is the substance of the Son, and the substance of the Spirit is the substance of both of them, then why are the Son and Spirit, in that they are Son and Spirit, particularities of the Father, rather than each of them being Father and the Father a particularity to them?[12]

Furthermore, for al-Baqillani, Jesus performed miracles similar to the manner that Moses also performed phenomenal miracles. Christians, however, claim that Moses prayed to God for signs whereas Jesus' miracles lay in his divinity. Al-Baqillani argues that Christians deny that Jesus too prayed to God for signs, and that if Jesus is divine in performing miracles, the same should be claimed for Moses. On the issue of substances, he put forward the challenge that if the Word united with the body of Christ, why did it not unite with the body of Moses or any of the other prophets? These kinds of questions by Muslims reflect a rationalist style of argument, taking the Christian defence seriously. However, they also reveal a complete reluctance to understand the Christian view of Jesus and the associated doctrines from a Christian logic and devotion.

Whichever period of history we explore, Christ's divinity and Muhammad's prophecy have continued to challenge both religions. For most Christians, Islam had no credibility as a true religion because Muhammad had no credibility as a true prophet; the Qur'an was not divine word simply because Muhammad claimed it to be. Christians were not interested in emphasising Jesus' role as a prophet, because that was not how they saw Christ. Rather, it is through Christ that humanity witnessed the fullness of God. In Islam, there is no divine accolade bigger than the election of prophecy, for the prophet/messenger is chosen to be close to God and to deliver God's message. But in Christianity, prophecy is not enough. The Hellenistic development of Christology, the councils of Nicaea and Chalcedon, pointed to a different truth, a truth which stated that Jesus was the Christ, the Word and the revelation of God. Even if Jesus' prophetic calling has been mentioned in the Bible, as in Luke 7:16, 'And there came a fear on all and they glorified God, saying, "A great prophet has risen up among us and God has visited his people,"' the prophetic nature does not express the deepest truth about him. In denying God's self-revelation in Christ, Muslims were denying the very nature of God. Muslims also reject that Jesus died on the cross and was resurrected, thus denying the paschal mystery. Despite his ascension and his return at the end times, neither the story of the crucifixion nor his return indicates a divine nature, redemption or salvation for humankind; even in his second coming he remains God's messenger only. Mahmoud Ayoub tries to portray what I call the 'something more' in Jesus:

> Like the Christ of Christian faith and hope, the Jesus of the Qur'an and later Muslim piety is much more than a mere human being, or even simply the messenger of a Book. While the Jesus of Islam

> is not the Christ of Christianity, the Christ of the Gospel often
> speaks through the austere, human Jesus of Muslim piety. Indeed,
> the free spirits of Islamic mysticism found in the man Jesus not
> only the example of piety, love and asceticism which they sought
> to emulate, but also the Christ who exemplifies fulfilled humanity,
> a humanity illumined by God.[13]

I have emphasised Christology as an important issue between Muslims and Christians because I cannot think of a more serious doctrinal debate between the two faiths. To engage in Christological debates requires a depth of understanding and openness on all sides. The Norwegian Lutheran minister and interreligious scholar Oddbjorn Leirvik writes that as a post-Christian religion which has included much of the Christian heritage, 'Islam challenges Christianity by competing in its own field'.[14] He argues against Christ being trapped inside the walls of the church because Jesus is a global figure who is also present in other non-Christian cultures.

But if Christian scholars are beginning to recognise the significance of Jesus as an interreligious figure, an image present in non-Christian cultures, how many Muslims will be willing to engage in serious Christology or any other Christian doctrine as a form of dialogue? And how many Christians will be concerned with what Muslims have to say on Christology? Christology may be only one factor in dialogue but it is an extremely important factor when both Christians and Muslims speak of God. One can well ask, how can Muslims and Christians talk about the same God when they hold such different understandings of the same God? I have heard many theologians struggle with the question of whether Muslims and Christians believe in the same God. For example, the Christian God loves unconditionally, the

Muslim God turns to you when you turn to him. During a lecture to a group of Catholic students in Rome two years ago, I was asked by a young nun, 'How do you Muslims know God loves you?' I asked her how she knew God loved her, to which she replied, 'Jesus died for us, that is how I know God loves me; his only son died for our sins.' This young nun spoke with conviction about her own beliefs and seemed to be genuinely sceptical as to how Muslims understand God's love when there is no distinctive event to reflect this love. For her, scripture was not enough, scriptural promises of God's love were not enough; rather, they were secondary to what God had done to himself to show love for his creation. For her, nothing in Islam compared to the doctrines of redemption and self-giving. This conversation has been one of several in which I have sensed that many Christians understand the concept of divine love as a central difference between Islam and Christianity. Not only is this often understood by clustering Islam and Judaism together, usually against Christianity, as religions of the law, more concerned with right practice than right doctrine, but this approach is further confirmed by acknowledging that while monotheistic traditions all speak of God's love, it is Christianity alone which speaks of God's unconditional love. The argument is that in Islam the kind of love which is manifested through the fulfilment of precepts and submission to God's will (*nomos*)[15] by its very nature speaks of a bilateral commitment between man and God. Here God loves when human beings obey. In contrast, Christianity is seen as a religion which is about God's love for man, not man's love for God. Here God loves irrespective of whether human beings obey.

There are other pronounced perceptions. Islam is bound by the limits of law, a kind of servile obedience, whereas

Christianity believes in God's unlimited love. Christianity stresses that God is understood to be acting in the course of human history, that God is sustaining the world through an act of will. In Islam, there is a sense that though God is near humanity and guides history, through his transcendence he is external to history. Observing some of the historical and present polemics between the two religions, once could legitimately ask if dialogue is not directed at conversion to Christ or to the event of the Qur'an, what is its real purpose? Yet even if we understand God's interaction with humanity in different ways, I would reply that constructive dialogue does not diminish one's faith but rather enlarges it. What we believe, how we listen to others and how we learn are part of the dialogue journey; we can be interested in learning for the sake of learning, for the hope of self-transformation, quite simply by trying to understand the many ways in which others feel God is a presence in their lives. Thus, I can accept one of the ways in which the Christian understanding of salvation is not determined by moral behaviour. Human beings are broken and need redemption. As C. S. Lewis writes, being good and nice does not mean that our souls are saved:

> For mere improvement is not redemption, though redemption always improves people even here and now, and will in the end improve them to a degree we cannot yet imagine. God became man to turn creatures into sons: not simply to produce better men of the old kind but to produce a new kind of man. It is not like teaching a horse to jump better and better but like turning a horse into a winged creature.[16]

Lewis stresses the Christian focus on human transformation, not just improvement. In the Christian tradition there is a sense of the tragedy of the human situation, which among other things asserts that sinful man has lost the knowledge of God against whom he has sinned and that God frees us from this ignorance and reveals to us both who he is and who we are. The human condition is one of a certain lostness and brokenness in which humanity is not able to save itself. Thus, 'The character, acts and teaching of Jesus, are seen as God's own revelatory and loving acts for our salvation.'[17] Much of the doctrinal polemics and apologetics in Christian–Muslim debates has continued to focus on how God is understood *as* revelation and also *through* revelation. Both religions recognise that there can be no adequate account of human experience without reference to God, but they see God's interaction with humanity in different ways. In Islam, human relations with God are conceptualised in the framework of servant to master. It is, in fact, one of the first questions asked by God: 'And when your Lord extracted from the children of Adam, from their spinal cord, their entire progeny and made them witness upon themselves, saying, "Am I not your Lord" and they replied, "No doubt you are we bear witness."' Nomanul Haq writes about the power of this narrative and its deep entrenchment in the Muslim consciousness: '[H]umanity in the very principle of its being has testified to the majesty of God. In other words, human nature is essentially theomorphic. To recognise God is to be in a natural state.'[18] Man's nature inclines him towards God and thus the servant–master (*abd–rabb*) relationship between man and God is a natural state, not a servile state. The significance of this relationship is that human beings cannot be understood on their own – only in the context of their relations with God. Yet there is still this mutuality, even dependency, between God and humanity, perhaps most poignantly expressed in a well-known hadith of untraceable origin: 'I was a hidden treasure and I yearned to be known. So I created creatures in order to be known by them.' This is a saying found mostly in the writings of the Sufi Ibn al-'Arabi. But why does God yearn to be known? Using this hadith to analyse the themes of sadness and identity found in the works of the Turkish writer Orhan Pamuk, Ian Almond writes, 'If Allah is a symptom of the unhappiness of the believer, then belief is also a product of the unhappiness of Allah; if God is an expression of our loneliness, then equally we are an expression of God's.'[19]

It is only in some of the classical Sufi poetry that we see images of Jesus which reflect a kind of sentiment that contrasts with the more prosaic doctrinal focus of the theologians. Ibn al-'Arabi refers to the sectarian disagreements over the nature of Jesus but it was the image of Jesus as divine spirit that is emphasised in his poetry:

> Considered in his [particular] mortal form, one might say that he is the son of Mary. Considered in his form of humanity, one might say that he is of Gabriel, while considered with respect to the revival of the dead one might say that he is of God as Spirit. Thus one might call him the spirit of God, which is to say that life is manifest into whomsoever he blows.[20]

But even mystical poetry did not reflect the full significance of Jesus' life with respect to his persecution, sacrifice and salvific presence. In the poetry of the thirteenth-century Turkish Persian mystic and poet/theologian, Jalal al-din Rumi, we find a variety of themes which dominated mystical poetry in its expressions about Jesus. Rumi is considered the greatest of the Persian poets and is certainly one of the most popular. His poetry presents different images of Jesus and Christianity. While he is less saviour and Son of God and more the Muslim prophet, Rumi sees Jesus as the smiling prophet and much more than a miracle worker. As a prophet, Jesus represents the perfection of humanity, a concept in which the attributes of God are mainfest. Rumi saw that logic and intellect were limited in their ability to inspire humanity to any great endeavour. It was the prophets and seers, people of no formal knowledge, who captured the hearts of those they met:

> The myriad of Pharaoh's lances were shattered by Moses with a single staff. Myriad were the therapeutic arts of Galen; before Jesus and his life giving breath they were a laughing stock. Myriad were the books of pre-Islamic poems; at the word of an illiterate prophet they were put to shame.

There are categories of understanding other than words:

> Our speech and action is the exterior journey: the interior journey is above the sky. The physical sense saw only dryness because it was born of earth: the Jesus of the spirit set foot on the sea.[21]

When looking even briefly at some of the doctrinal and poetic literature, it seems strange to many audiences that the Islamic world that for so long had such a rigorous intellectual outlook and so many contacts with other religions, today displays relatively little interest in the history and doctrines of other faiths. I understand this as a contemporary intellectual gap in the Islamic world, but many Muslim scholars see this as reflecting the inner universalism of Islam. For example, Seyyed Hossein Nasr writes:

> The reason for this relative neglect of the discipline of comparative religion by Muslims is that Islam is not at all disturbed theologically by the presence of other religions. The

existence of other religion is taken for granted and in fact Islam is
based on the conception of the universality of revelation.[22]

This is an easy interpretation to make if we look at certain
verses of the Qur'an which speak of the existence of other
faiths and the recognition of other communities, namely
Christianity and Judaism, as in this example:

> Indeed those who believe and those who are Jews and the Sabeans
> and the Christians are those who believe in God and the last day
> and righteous deeds, so they have their recompense with God.
> They shall not fear nor shall they sorrow. (Q2:62)

Also, the Qur'an states that 'To every people we have sent a
messenger, that they may worship God' to draw attention to
the universalism of prophecy as being God's chosen method
of conveying his divine message in human history. Yet
alongside such verses are also those verses which have been
interpreted as more exclusivist in tone, as for example, 'Who
seeks other than Islam as a religion, it will not be accepted
from him' (Q3:85). In writing about the verses which
advocate tolerance and acceptance of other people, which
first drew him to Islam, Joseph Lumbard notes that 'despite a
clear message of universality, tolerance and pluralism in the
Qur'an, the main theological line and hermeneutic traditions
have almost always chosen to read the universal, inclusivist
dimension of the Qur'an, and of the sayings of the Prophet
Muhammad in light of more exclusivist verses ... These are
trumpeted in many quarters as incontrovertible evidence
that only those who follow the Prophet Muhammad shall be
saved.'[23] Thus, it seems to me that if the exclusivist verses
have been interpreted more literally than the inclusivist
verses, then Muslims have to some extent not been

'theologically disturbed' by the existence of other religions because they have quite simply dismissed their relevance. One could feasibly argue that most Muslims do not study other religions or argue against other religions not because they recognise them as true in some way but because they do not regard them as relevant after the coming of Islam. Joseph Lumbard argues against this view with a quote from the thirteenth-century Imam Nawawi:

> Someone who does not believe that whoever follows another religion besides Islam is an unbeliever (like Christians), or doubts that such a person is an unbeliever, or considers their sect to be invalid, is himself an unbeliever [kafir] even if he manifests Islam and believes in it.[24]

But despite such sayings, the majority of the Islamic exegetical tradition has preferred the exclusivist reading of verses relating to other revealed religions. In the same anthology, William Chittick analyses the Sufi master Ibn al-ʿArabi's rejection of a common view that the coming of Islam abrogated previous revealed religions. Chittick provides the following quote from Ibn al-ʿArabi in which Islam is like the sun and the other religions are like the stars:

> All the revealed religions are like lights. Among these religions, the revealed religion of Muhammad is like the light of the sun among the lights of the stars. When the sun appears, the lights of the stars are hidden, and their lights are included in the light of the sun. Their being hidden is like the abrogation of the other revealed religions that takes place through Muhammad's revealed religion. Nevertheless, they do in fact exist, just as the existence of the light of the stars is actualized. This explains why we have been required in all our all-inclusive religion to have faith in the truth of all the messengers and the revealed religions. They are

not rendered null (*batil*) by abrogation – that is the opinion of
the ignorant.[25]

These scholarly views argue for a kind of universalism in
Islam which must be open to other revealed faiths, but it
is difficult to measure the impact of such views on Muslim
societies. Much of the dialogical work today focuses on the
importance of understanding one's own faith within the
context of the wider world and global perspectives where
inter-religious discussions matter as much as intra-religious.
Both Islam and Christianity have been informed by a sort
of religious plurality from the beginning, but the issue of
religious pluralism – simply being aware and challenged by
how to embrace or exclude other religious communities – is
present in a new way today. It has led many scholars who see
themselves articulating a theology of religions to assert that
however much we talk of truth within our own religion, we
cannot talk of a singular truth. Islam and Christianity, as the
two largest faiths in the world, have a particular stake in this
debate, which has a political as well as theological urgency. I
say political because many now recognise that over the last 15
years or so, especially after the attacks of 11 September 2001,
there has been a shift in the way Islam is viewed – namely
as a political and not just a religious threat to the West. It
took the tragedy of 9/11 and the subsequent phenomenon of
jihadist rhetoric and terrorism to create a new global political
tension. It seems to me that 9/11 is not just another date. For
some in the West, it has become a symbol of a fundamental
tension, a symbol of all that is good in the West against all
that is bad in the Muslim world. This is partly because we
tend to replace the concept of Christian and Muslim with the
West and Islam – as if the two meant the same thing. Thus
Islam becomes a religion, culture and civilisation opposed

to liberal values which are seen as Western. I don't believe in this polarised debate in which Islam and the West appear to be two separate entities. Muslims for their part conflate Christian with Western, and thus any issues they have with European or Western governments and their foreign policies are often erroneously confused with the Christian faith. Just as many Christians are struggling with the gradual decline of religiosity in public life in much of Western Europe, the Muslim world is struggling with the growing narrowness of its own attitudes to others, often deliberately combining the Christian religion with the Western powers to produce an emotive and intolerant narrative. Religion and politics conjure up powerful emotions, and Samuel Huntington's potent but too often misused phrase, 'clash of civilisations', emerged as the term favoured in the media and politics to distinguish the Islamic world from the rest of the world.

This has been a particular concern in the wake of the invasion of Iraq and Afghanistan. But the post-9/11 world has also seen a rise in anti-Islamic polemical literature, insisting that Islam is essentially a violent religion and that Christians should rise to the defence of Christianity against the increasing Islamisation of Western lands. There is evidence of some groups of Christian evangelicals in America stressing that there is little common ground between Christianity and Islam, and that Islam is not only a violent religion but also a wicked religion. In September 2010, an American Pentecostal pastor in Florida named Terry Jones made global headlines when he planned to burn a hundred of copies of the Qur'an on the anniversary of the attack on the Twin Towers in New York in September 2001. He drew widespread condemnation, including from President Barack Obama, the Vatican and General David Petraeus, then the US military commander in

Afghanistan. Jones ultimately cancelled the event, though he
did burn one copy of the Qur'an in spring 2010, sparking
deadly riots in Afghanistan. Jones's anger stemmed from his
belief that Islam is a religion of the devil which does not
teach that Jesus is the son of God and which articulates a
despicable ideology. He argued that America should not allow
itself to be controlled by radical Islam and that the Qur'an
burning was a reflection of his anger at the growing spread of
Islam. I gave a speech at the time about this incident, quoting
Ralph Emerson who said that 'Every book burned enlightens
the world.' Emerson was right, for a book burning is never
simply about a book burning, but rather reflects a world of a
simmering fury and demands that we re-evaluate who we are
as people, states and communities.

This kind of prejudice is not so much ethnically or racially
motivated, as it is directed against the religion of Islam.[26]
In his work on anti-Islamic polemics, Cimino argues that
many former Muslims who have converted to Christianity
are keen to reveal the 'truth' about Islam, which they argue
encourages violence and extremism as tenets of the Qur'an.
Thus the God of the Christians and the God of the Muslims
cannot be the same.

Despite the wars and conflicts which arose in the aftermath
of these tragic events, 9/11 stands out as an iconic image of a
very modern conflict and a metaphor for all that we had failed
to foresee about the lethal mix of religion and politics. What
this event did was to convince many onlookers that religious
expression could quite easily be equated with religious
fanaticism, and that Muslim fanaticism was essentially an
anti-Western force. The sound of medieval Qur'anic verses
combined with the roar of a crashing modern jet plane didn't
just bring death and destruction but brought it in the name

of a God and scripture held sacred by millions. People would often ask, 'Did 9/11 change your life?' I would reply, not really, but as a Muslim I was at times expected to explain the rhetoric of terror and militancy. Even sophisticated theological debates between Muslims and Christians often focused on only one point – was the Muslim God loving like the Christian God? Suddenly we were all experts on all kinds of geopolitical issues simply by virtue of our faith, because Islam was now no longer the second largest faith in the world, but was also seen by some as the biggest threat to world peace.

A few years ago a colleague remarked jokingly, '9/11 has been good for your career.' I wondered whether that was true. I have never jumped on the political bandwagon that followed these attacks but was it easier to speak of religion at a time of conflict rather than peace? Did conflict keep God contested but alive in our society? Yet, years on, there's been a shift in the way we in Western Europe talk of the Islamic presence. Our language has turned from militancy to values. Do Muslim societies share the values of pluralist liberal democracies? This debate is about ethics and the spread of a more singular kind of narrative about normative, liberal values which are now seen as the essential context for human freedom.

The recent conflict in Syria, and in many parts of the Middle East where there is sectarian Sunni–Shi'a killing, have also compounded Christian–Muslim tensions, as Christians have increasingly become targets of anti-Western Muslim sentiment. Christian churches and communities have been attacked as part of the political posturing between pro-government and anti-government forces. Though the uprising in Syria began primarily to end the authoritarian reign of President Bashar al-Assad, for many in the opposition movement the aim has become the creation of an Islamic state, governed by a harsh interpretation of Islamic law and free of any Christian presence.[27] While there are stories of Christians and Muslims protecting each other as ancient neighbourly communities, the escalation of violence against some Christian communities has created a new political tension which inevitably plays out in the West's image of Islam as a whole. As a Muslim colleague bemoaned at the 2014 World Economic Forum meeting in Davos, Muslim leaders suffer from an 'epistemic arrogance' and appear to have lost all sense of humility, unable to understand the very concept of power sharing.

In December 2013, I took part in a 'Christianity and Religious Freedom' conference in Rome where the Chaldean Patriarch of Iraq gave a speech on what the Middle East would lose if the Christians left.[28] He spoke movingly at times and stated that it was the Christian presence that would guarantee Muslims a better life. It was an intriguing and probably true statement to make because religious diversity requires understanding, patience and the willingness to engage with society in particular ways; diversity alone does not mean social pluralism. I thought to myself whether it was even possible to imagine the Middle East without the Christian presence there in all its diversity and with its pre-Islamic heritage. How could these lands be stripped bare of those who have lived and worshipped there, whose ancestors are buried there and whose very souls belong there? I am sure that many Christians and Muslims in times of conflict offer support to each other as neighbours and friends. But if the political unrest in so many of these countries resulted in a divisive and harsh form of Islamic rule, the diminishing presence and possible loss of Christian communities should be seen as a scandal to the Muslim conscience.

At another conference in Germany in January 2014, which looked at religion and public space, a Palestinian Christian pastor spoke about the situation in Jerusalem and Bethlehem. He bemoaned the fact that while Western Europe may be going through its own crisis of secularism, his own lands had 'too much religion in public'. Muslim headscarves were becoming more common, Christian crosses were becoming larger, and liturgies across the religions were becoming louder and lengthier. Religious visibility did not mean a deeper faith – quite the opposite. The politicisation of religion as a marker of identity and otherness is creating new and more dangerous kinds of expressions where the public space is an increasingly contested space.

In fact much of the unrest and violence in the Middle East also points to another most unsettling fact – the increasing instability of so many Muslim countries. In 2013, thousands of Egyptians staged a six-week sit-in, demanding the reinstatement of the Islamist leader Muhammad Morsi. After conflict broke out, with Egyptian killing Egyptian, many proclaimed that they would die for their freedom and be prepared to shed their blood for Islam. As I heard these words, it seemed to me that many Islamic countries, despite enjoying the cultural and more secular lifestyles of the West, always use the most divisive religious rhetoric to wound rather than heal their countries. The readiness to die, to kill and to create unrest may be real for them in the passion of the moment but notwithstanding the genuine concerns ordinary people have in many Islamic states, the consequences of this rhetoric are never limited to one country alone. Hardliners, Islamists, liberals and progressives are all forced to sit somewhere on the religious spectrum and all of us in the West watch at a safe but precarious distance.

Added to this are events which make global news and only serve to confirm in the minds of many that Islam is an intolerant religion. One such incident occurred in September 2012 when a Pakistani Christian teenage girl, Rimsha Masih, who had learning difficulties, was taken into custody after angry mobs alleged that she had burnt or desecrated pages inscribed with verses from the Qur'an. In Pakistan, such allegations often fall under the umbrella of the country's blasphemy laws, resulting in calls for draconian punishments against Christians and other minorities. The strange twist to this case, however, came a few days later when a Muslim cleric, Khalid Chishti, was accused and later arrested for implanting burnt pages of the Qur'an himself in the girl's bag because as one witness says, he wanted to expel the Christian community from the locality. The subsequent response by other Muslim clerics calling for justice for the girl was almost unprecedented in a country which has acquired a reputation for extremism and intolerance. Islam is the state religion in Pakistan, and in 1986 the penal code introduced under article 295 C, various kinds of punishments including the death penalty for blasphemy against the Prophet. Blasphemy laws are an extreme form of social control, leaving many minority religious communities constantly fearful of the government irrespective of how infrequently punishments are actually carried out. In 2010, the Muslim governor of the Punjab, Salman Taseer, was killed because he publicly defended the revision of such laws. Over the last couple of years, there have been increased attacks on churches in many parts of the Muslim world including Pakistan. In 2013, over 70 people were killed and 130 injured in one of the deadliest bomb attacks on a historic church in Peshawar. Writing about the Christian minority in Pakistan, the former diplomat Akbar Ahmad said that there was a time when Christians were very much part of the fabric of the nation but that now amidst increasing public disorder, they had become extremely vulnerable and persecuted:

> Many Pakistanis are unaware of the role Christians have played in the nation's history. Although the Christian population is barely three million, or 1.6 percent of the population – as compared with 180 million Muslims (more than 95 percent) – Christians have had a considerable impact, especially in education. Many of Pakistan's most prominent leaders – including the current prime minister, Nawaz Sharif, the assassinated prime minister, Benazir Bhutto, and former President Pervez Musharraf – went to Christian schools. Christians also educated Muhammad Ali Jinnah, who founded Pakistan in 1947. Under Pakistan's Constitution, Christians were guaranteed equal rights.[29]

Such cases are a lethal mix of religion and politics, but they show how we in the West struggle to understand how societies can show this lack of compassion and allow the abuse of human rights, all in the name of Islam. But Rimsha's case also affirmed that human rights for all is not an embattled cliché of the last 50 years. Rather, it remains a universal struggle often highlighted by the plight of a single individual, and in our age of instant global communication, no country can hide either the individual or the injustice from the rest of the world.

It is precisely because there is so much civil conflict that can be exacerbated through religious tension that we need engaged voices at every level. Thus there is no one way to engage in dialogue because dialogue involves and affects religion, politics and civil society. It looks different in peaceful societies and one may legitimately wonder whether it serves any real purpose for change in areas of real conflict where people are killed simply because of their faith. But it seems to me that we have no alternative to speaking and acting together. Religious difference is only one form of difference and hardly ever the only reason behind murderous conflict. Yet, religious language is the most potent kind of language and now used ubiquitously to defend all kinds of fanaticism. In 2005, Abdou Filali-Ansary wondered why we follow fundamentalists who use religious language to add legitimacy to their perspectives:

> Today it is clear that fundamentalists and their supporters are completely closed off to even the most elaborate theological refutation of their views, even when produced by distinguished religious authorities. The first reflex of the fundamentalists is to withdraw from the mainstream, to build around themselves a shell that is impervious to any logic except their own. The most essential questions that humans face today – those that engender the deepest conflicts – have nothing to do with theology. They concern disputes over territory, political power, definition of rights and distribution of wealth. The means of discussing these questions is known to all and is expressed in all religions and all languages.[30]

I am assured in my faith in God and also remain assured that our faith is never weakened only enlarged through questioning and self-reflection. I don't engage in dialogue to 'sell' my understanding of God or to attempt to shake someone else's faith. I would hope that this approach is shared by most dialogue participants even though I have experienced moments of frustration at the rigidity and lack of hospitality in some colleagues. Many years ago, at an interfaith conference, a Catholic priest kept shaking his head in despair as he repeatedly came up to me and sighed, 'If only you Muslims would get rid of the law.' It seemed strange to me that someone who knew little if anything about the complexities of the law in Islam, saw it as a simple obstacle between human beings and God. A few years ago I had a conversation with a Roman Catholic archbishop who was also a good friend. He spoke to me about the necessity of dialogue for human friendship but added that while mission may not be at the forefront of most contemporary dialogue, the spirit of mission could not be absent from such conversations. He added, 'At some point, I would hope you too are moved by the Spirit.' I admit to having felt slightly dismayed at what was being implied, but also wondered why this moral imperative of mission bothered me. Yet recently, while speaking in the Netherlands, a Catholic theologian and friend told me of his own concerns regarding conversion, concluding in a way that was both surprising and comforting. He explained how a friend of his wanted to convert to Catholicism but the theologian was hesitant, even reluctant, to explore this journey with him. When I pressed him as to why he felt like this, he replied, 'When my friend said he wanted to convert, it was kind of frightening, as if all of this might really be true.' It seemed to me that most of us spend so much time thinking and writing about religion and theology that we face the danger of becoming distant from the living realities and dimensions of faith in God. Thus, when someone else perceives a glimpse of the divine in our lives, we are silenced in awe of the power and grace which has brought about this experience. Such stories may be personal anecdotes but they convey something of the unexpected gift that is faith, a gift which transforms us from within. As far as Muslim colleagues are concerned, I have witnessed a genuine change in many of those who came into dialogue with suspicion and even condescension towards their Christian counterparts. Over the years, these same people began to understand their dialogue partners not as threats but as friends who shared a desire to talk about God and who believed that it is our relationship with God which really gives meaning to our lives.

As a Muslim who has lived most of her life in the West, I have learnt that faith speaks to faith in many ways. Dialogue has been a process of learning and accepting, of questioning and appreciating, of self-doubt and humility. Most importantly, it has been to understand that talking about a common humanity demands much generosity in the face of practical difference. Engaging in dialogue is an extension of *ihsan* for me, 'To Act knowing that even if you cannot see God, he can see you.' Thus, I sit with Christian theologians who are friends, who are challenging, who are suspicious, and with those who are just willing to talk. Personally, I am not interested in pluralism, exclusivism or inclusivism as philosophical systems to work within. My interest lies primarily in the diversity of theological debates that both traditions have about human nature, divine nature and the eternal question of the relationship between God and man. We should always feel that we can remain open to thinking about God in new ways. As the Qur'an itself says:

> And if all the trees on earth were pens and the oceans [were ink], with seven oceans behind it to add, yet the words of God will not be exhausted; for God is exalted in power, full of wisdom. (Q37:27)

It seems to me, however, that ultimately dialogue is enriched by theological debate but its true value lies in our ethical approaches to one another. When we reflect on God we also reflect on human ethics and the kind of relationships which make for a more flourishing society for all. Thus when dialogue works it is because of the commitment of individuals to see something beyond their own world, their own comfort, to face a challenge that has its own risks but where the end value is about a commitment to bring something affirmative to society. Self-satisfaction can never bring about a good society and most of us recognise that our bonds with one another form the essential basis for civilisation.

In *Civilisation and its Discontents*, Freud argued that the strongest defence against human aggressiveness is the religious commandment to love one's neighbour as oneself. It is justified by the fact that 'nothing else runs so much counter to basic human nature'.[31] The harder it is to follow this commandment, the more meritorious it is to do so. The difficulty lies in the fact that this call is the most contrary to the kind of reason which civilisation promotes: aggressiveness and the selfish pursuit of happiness. Bauman, however, contends:

> Accepting the precept of loving one's neighbour is the birth act of humanity. All other routines of human cohabitation, as well as their predesigned or retrospectively discovered rules, are but a (never complete) list of footnotes to that precept. Were this precept to be ignored or thrown away, there would be no one to make that list or ponder its completeness.

Self-love is necessary for survival but 'loving one's neighbour as one loves oneself makes *human* survival unlike the survival of any living creatures'.[32]

Today, belief in God is for most people a personal choice, even if it is viewed as an act of grace. However, I think that once we have committed ourselves to talking about a God who is merciful and loving, a God who intercedes in human history, then we are obliged to rethink not just who we are as people of faith but also what does our faith mean when it comes to engaging with others. When someone stands in front of me, I have the option of listening, holding my hand out in friendship or simply turning away. If we are living in the presence of God, we need to believe in ourselves and in others that our faiths and cultures can have a positive impact and work for the welfare of the wider society, the public good. Silence here is not an option, faith here is not something to be hidden but must be open and generous, especially if it means facing our own fears and prejudices. Our creeds and convictions are intrinsic to our identities but every relationship we have with one another reflects in some way our covenant with God. Life is a series of encounters in which God is always present.

In areas where personal and communal conflict comes to define people's identities, action is everything. In peaceful societies, words matter not because lives are at stake but because how we speak of our faith says something about ourselves. We need to be reminded that there are silences we keep out of respect for ourselves and others, but there are also silences we keep out of fear. Today there are too many people who fear, too many who think they are victims and too many who think that things will simply get better of their own accord. When I think of why it is important to be actively involved in religious work, engaged with both dialogue or praxis, it is fundamentally because each of us will leave a legacy for our children who continue to live in a world of varying conflicts. As parents and scholars, we have the ability in some small way to influence this legacy and we have the moral duty to do so. For the faithful, religions are divine in origin but they are largely built around the narratives we've chosen, the stories we tell to keep us connected to the sacred. The wisdom of the prophets and saints have been kept alive because their words inspire, they lift us out of the ordinary so that we can see that for all that we do, there's always so much more we can do. Islam is a faith which began with the command to speak, to recite in the name of God; it is a religion built around the eloquence of scripture, the power of the pen and the encouragement to reflect upon life – this is a fundamental Qur'anic message. Nothing is more challenging than the command to live the good life with ourselves and our neighbours, to have hope in the future of all communities despite the uncertainties and vulnerabilities of our lives. This is an absolute imperative based on the consolation that as human beings we are moral beings who have always been concerned with what it is to be human. As Hannah Arendt writes:

> The world is not humane just because it is made by human beings, and it does not become humane just because the human voice sounds in it, but only when it has become the object of discourse. However much we are affected by the things of the world, however deeply they may stir and stimulate us, they become human for us only when we can discuss them with our fellows ... we humanize what is going on in the world and in ourselves only by speaking of it, and in the course of speaking of it we learn to be human. The Greeks called this humanness which is achieved in the course of friendship *philanthropia*, 'love of man', since it manifests itself in a readiness to share the world with other men.[33]

There is no nihilism in Islam despite the nihilistic rhetoric which has characterised the contentious term 'political Islam' today. Politics and religion both divide; both can arouse intense passions, contempt or apathy. But religion and politics are fundamental, albeit in different ways, to nations and societies. Thus, each of us has choices on how to live and act notwithstanding social and political conflicts; we have the opportunity to create new histories based on hope and humility in our openness to others. Conflict may always be part of the human condition but there are no limits to what the phrase 'our common humanity' can achieve.

FIVE

Religion, Multiculturalism and the Public Space

Was my generation the generation which defined multiculturalism? Was our integration into British society part of some political experiment? It seems such a long time ago since the 1970s and 1980s when I was growing up as a second-generation Muslim quite unaware of the social changes and political dynamics which had established the concept of multiculturalism as Britain's future. Whatever else the word means, at the very least multiculturalism is understood to be a respect for diverse ways of living within the same society. But respect itself is open to various interpretations, including levels of tolerance, acceptance and understanding. Nevertheless it is premised on an acceptance of various colours, cuisines and cultures as part of the fabric of society, notwithstanding any tensions that might ensue from people actually living and working together. In 2005, Alan Cowell commented in the Europe section of the *New York Times*:

> True, these days, Britain has the look – far more than many other European nations – of a land that has come to terms with the notion that its ethnic diversity is permanent. Black and Asian anchors and journalists read and report the television news.

Parliament boasts a sprinkling of nonwhite lawmakers. The 30,000-plus Metropolitan Police in London, once virtually all white, is slowly making way for nonwhite officers: 7 percent of the force is currently made up of nonwhites and the proportion in training is 17 percent. The police shows on television feature black officers.[1]

Even if we claim that this quote speaks more about ethnic visibility than anything else more specific, the word multiculturalism has become so contested today that it is seen by some as the failure of the past and the impasse of the future. It is tied to a particular kind of migration story, the successes and failures of which are only now becoming apparent. Twenty-five years ago, multiculturalism was defined through food and festivals, especially the Indian takeaway; today it is examined through the prism of terror and human rights. This is especially so with relation to the diverse Muslim presence in the UK.

My parents came to Britain in the late 1960s without attaching any theological or political importance to the question of migration. For them, it was essentially about wanting a better life and better education for their children. They managed to find a way of coexistence in society which challenged them at times but in no way made them feel less Muslim or less *as* Muslims. So, when I was growing up, the concept of multiculturalism was not really discussed, even if it was the political and social context of the 1970s and 1980s. We lived as British citizens who practised a culture that maintained aspects of the subcontinent and understood in some unspoken way what Britishness meant. Issues around food, clothing, personal laws of marriage and divorce hardly made headline news, and multiculturalism just seemed to be happening around us. Despite occasional tensions, I can't remember feeling any particular angst or viewing multiculturalism as making competing claims on my identity. There was no choice but to live with multiple identities and loyalties. A person's identity is not static or singular; rather, identities are created over time, something that as individuals we grow into or become through our relationships and interactions with society around us. In exploring the multiple dimensions of his own Arab Christian identity, Amin Maalouf describes a sense of allegiances inherent in the concept, a sense that our identity is acquired step by step, yet is something which we experience as a complete whole:

> A person's identity is not an assemblage of separate affiliations, nor a kind of loose patchwork; it is like a pattern drawn on a tightly stretched parchment. Touch just one part of it, just one allegiance and the whole person will react, the whole drum will sound.[2]

That there exist cultural differences between the various minority groups in the UK has been accepted for the last 50 years; indeed that was the vaguely defined ethos of multiculturalism. But 9/11 and the London bombings of 2005 branded multiculturalism a failure and in particular the Islamic component of multiculturalism. It was thought that the bombings were the result of a deep malaise amongst many second- or third-generation Muslims who felt no loyalty to Britain. The question amongst the population at large and the policymakers was whether Muslims hold different values that will inevitably clash with the values of liberal democracies and civil societies of the West. When you add words such as 'extremism' or 'radicalism' and they gradually become part of everyday language, whole communities are then seen quite simply as a problem. Several years ago at a conference in Berlin, the German Minister of the Interior commented cryptically to me, 'Since the demise of the wall, Islam is the biggest issue in Germany.' He was not referring to legal issues around nationality, and so on, for minorities in Germany, nor to the existence of cultural differences between the various minorities which has been allowed to exist in Germany and indeed most of Western Europe for the last 50 years. Rather, the issue at hand was the question of values – the values European citizens live by. If it was true, as was being implied, that Muslims do hold different values, then what values could form the basis of the public and private spaces of civil society?

The problem with talking about communities in any politicised manner is that the discussion tends to view minority groups as monolithic in their identity and self-expression. A minority but significant religion in the West, Islam has recently come under fierce criticism as a faith which nurtures intolerant theological orientations, and its frequent clashes with the freedoms of the West is seen to be based on a stringent adherence to the isolationist principles of shari'a. Here the recent focus on citizenship has assumed a new urgency as to how governments can create and nurture a sense of citizenship amongst ethnic groups and especially amongst Muslims. In the classical Islamic theological and juridical literature, the changing political contexts demanded an appraisal of what constituted right belief and right action on matters where loyalty to faith might conflict with loyalty to the state. But today the issue of citizenship has become politically charged as a result of a growing perception that many people are just citizens of a state by birth but feel no engagement with society as a whole – not just in terms of political participation but in their sense of emotional belonging. I would argue that most Muslims living in Britain do feel this to be their home, at least the only home they know. For those who don't feel Britain is their home, there is a much deeper question about the real compatibility of very different cultures, and their ability to live in any meaningful way side by side. People may share a neighbourhood but they share little in terms of thoughts or activities. There may be no resentment, no hostility, but instead apathy. One could also argue that tolerance of difference does not make the difference more palatable. Britain is not multicultural if that implies equal living cultures – there are dominant 'white' cultures which can also often live worlds apart, and there are a variety of subcultures. While no culture remains frozen, the subcultures are prone to become more entrenched under the conviction that this is the right path for religious and cultural self-preservation. Even when new directions emerge from these subcultures, as within the Muslim minorities, the experience of life as a minority in a context of political and cultural pluralism often remains a novelty. For some, in their efforts to practise Islam in Europe, problems are encountered that previously were either unexamined or not systematically formulated in Islamic thought.

Thus it seems to me that despite its primacy as the fundamental political structure in society and its vast reach, the state remains limited in scope and operations with regard to the dynamics of social relations. So if I feel myself to be a British citizen then why do I feel this? Despite the theoretical frameworks which can be postulated about migration and citizenship, I would argue that essentially culture is more than holding onto food, dress and ritual. Cultural awareness and feelings of belonging demand a mindset, an ability to have a vision for your life wherever you live, to be aware of your heritage but not be burdened or held back by traditions that encourage only imaginary rather than real bonds. For me, citizenship is not simply tied to having the right passport or being able to vote, but in essence is about the feeling of belonging – I need to feel that I belong to a place so that I want to contribute to it with my thoughts, my words and my actions. The sense that my local, even national, context is one where I can make a difference involves action and engagement not passivity or apathy. This is particularly so in democracies which can flourish – indeed are strengthened – only when individual participation is encouraged and when critical thinking is allowed in private and public space without fear or threat.

Multiculturalism means different things to different people, but most Asian Muslims living in Britain by their own choice or parental choice still have links with the subcontinent. This should not be a test of loyalty or allegiance – it is just the way things are in a globalised age where communication, travel and diversity are all applauded. Relations with a homeland continue at a psychological, financial and sometimes political level; this relationship bridges both time and space. There is no one way or right way to be multicultural because the concept is as much about personal and individual choice as it is a loose political narrative. When my children were in primary school, a Muslim acquaintance of mine asked me a little accusingly 'Aren't you putting your children into an Islamic school?' I replied no, because the thought had never entered my head, and I wondered afterwards why that was so; indeed, why I was actually quite opposed to it. I realised that for me education and religion were two different territories:

yes, they may occasionally overlap but home was where my children learnt about their own faith and school was where they could put some of the teachings of the faith and upbringing into practice among people of all religions and none. If this exposed them to some discrimination, even to some derision, then so be it; it would be the test of how committed they were to their own religion but also how open they were to other ways of thinking.

The question for me is whether we as a society have understood how diversity is inherently a good thing and whether people of very different cultures really can live together in a meaningful way. This debate has acquired a new focus today, with questions raised about the place of religion in public life and more specifically the place of Islam in liberal democracies. I propose that this is essentially a debate about ethics rather than religious truths. I think the issue of ethics and normative ethics for multicultural, multi-perspective societies is one of the biggest challenges to communities who feel that the earth is shifting from beneath their feet and that they need to find some solid ground. Apart from a handful of works, classical Islam did not have systematic treatises on ethics, as the subject was subsumed under law and worship. The juridical literature gives us some insight as to the dilemma of whether Muslims could actively participate in non-Islamic societies, but these pre-modern texts are not conclusive by any means. More importantly, they do not contain within themselves the appropriate equivalent of words like 'liberalism', 'human rights' or 'democratic pluralism' – the global vocabulary of the modern age. With new contexts emerges a new language, and one of the biggest challenges for many Muslims who reflect on these issues is the alignment of text to context.

Tradition and orthodoxy are unthought, unelaborated concepts in Islamic classical thought. As the late Muhammad Arkoun argues, Muslim scholars need to 'initiate a process of new thinking on Islam with tools such as history of thought rather than political events or fixed parameters; to make unthinkable notions – a historical rather than a religious postulate – thinkable; and to relate secularism, religion, and culture to contemporary challenges rather than substituting one for the other'. For Arkoun, Islam as revelation is only one attempt to emancipate human beings from the natural limitations of their biological, historical and linguistic condition. In his critique of the varying polemics recently directed against Orientalism, Arkoun argued that what intellectual Islam needs today is a new epistemological perspective for the comparative study of cultures:

> So-called modern scholarship remains far from any epistemological project that would free Islam from the essentialist, substantialist postulates of classical meta-physics. Islam, in these discussions, is assumed to be a specific, essential, unchangeable system of thought, beliefs, and non-beliefs, one which is superior or inferior (according to Muslims or non-Muslims) to the Western (or Christian) system. It is time to stop this irrelevant confrontation between two dogmatic attitudes – the theological claims of believers and the ideological postulates of positivist rationalism.

For Arkoun, however limited the influence of intellectual writers might be in injecting new dynamism into Islamic thought, where traditions have a long and deeply rooted history, this enterprise is necessary. Furthermore, it must be the project of thinkers, writers, artists, scholars and economic producers. They must all be committed to the idea that 'thoughts have their own force and life. Some, at least, could survive and break through the wall of uncontrolled beliefs and dominating ideologies.'³ The project of thinking Islam is basically a response to two major needs: 1) the particular need of Muslim societies to think, for the first time, about their own problems which had been made unthinkable by the triumph of orthodox scholastic thought; and 2) the need of contemporary thought in general to open new fields and discover new horizons of knowledge, through a systematic cross-cultural approach to the fundamental problems of human existence. Arkoun is right because it seems to me that Muslim thinking on so many issues has historically been confined to interpretations, albeit varying, from the classical sources. Yet modern social and political complexities require bold new ways of thinking about dramatically different frameworks of life. This approach does not advocate disregarding the traditional sources but it does entail reviving them in new ways which keep them meaningful to contemporary concerns in all areas of life.

A very brief consideration of the history of the Islamic and then European expansion shows how Muslim countries were shaped and influenced by European powers. Islam expanded from what is now Saudi Arabia across North Africa, through the Middle East and into Asia and Europe. Historically, Islam in its diverse forms has been the religious ideology behind the foundation of a variety of Muslim states, including the great Islamic empires: Umayyad (661–750), Abbasid (750–1258), Ottoman (1281–1924), Safavid (1501–1722) and Mughal (1526–1857). By the eleventh century, the Islamic world was under attack from the Turks and the Mongols. They were not conquered by Islam; rather, they entered the Islamic world as conquerors and converted to Islam over the following centuries. However, the Europeans who came in the nineteenth and twentieth centuries to militarily colonise the Muslim world did not convert like the Turks and Mongols, which meant that for the first time Muslims were politically subjugated by the empires of Russia, Holland, Britain and France. The twentieth century was marked by two dominant themes: European colonialism and the Muslim struggle for independence. The legacy of colonialism remains alive today because colonialism altered the geographical map of the Muslim world by drawing the boundaries of the Muslim countries. After World War Two, the French were in West and North Africa, Lebanon and Syria; the British in Palestine, Iraq, the Persian Gulf, the Indian subcontinent, Malaya and Brunei; and the Dutch in Indonesia. European colonialism and its aftermath drastically changed the basis and the nature of political and social organisations within and among territorial states where all Muslims live today. Against this background, the migration of Muslims from different part of the Islamic world to European countries in the 1950s onwards was the first time that large groups of Muslims voluntarily left Muslim countries, bringing with them many of their cultural norms, to live in the West; this movement and migration was unprecedented in Europe. A couple of generations later, this original migration has assumed a variety of cultural patterns, and ethnic communities live culturally and religiously diverse lives. However, to view the Muslim presence as either an ethnic presence or a religious force separate from mainstream society perpetuates a narrow but powerful debate about civil society and indeed about globalism and civil society. The emergence of civil society in the course of European civilisation had been associated with liberal philosophy, which pits religious faith against the rational. This is a world where the individual is at the centre, and so a truly civil society cannot develop where the sacred encroaches on the public arena. This perspective simplifies, even caricatures, the sacred as competing in its claims on civil society rather than being one part of many parts of civil society.

Today, one of the key features of modernity is globalisation. Although globalisation has been seen largely in economic terms since the 1980s, the term incorporates the sense that global capitalism has been incorporating the world's regions into a single system. Whether this has a homogenising effect on cultures and lifestyles is debatable, but it has led to a global flow of ideas from all parts of the world. Globalisation also implicates religion in different ways, in that faiths often identify themselves in opposition to one another, creating or at least encouraging a kind of religious pluralism. Religions are less rooted in one place and there is a greater hybridity of religious expression because of diaspora lifestyles, networks and other international links, and thus religious communities must be seen as part of this ongoing pluralism integral to the process of globalisation.

Pluralism has become a focus of theological, social and political debate, a central point in our discussion of civil societies, often crossing boundaries of gender, race and religious minorities. Much of the discourse around it within Islamic studies, however, is not so much concerned with any systematic Qur'anic exegesis as it is with a selection of verses from the Qur'an which have been used to argue for an inherent Qur'anic endorsement and ideal of pluralist societies. These verses are used by scholars to argue that religious and thus civil pluralism is not an ideal but the only social and political framework envisaged in the Qur'an for good societies. Verses commonly used as a defence for religious pluralism are:

> O humankind, we have created you male and female, and appointed
> you races and tribes, that you may know one another. Surely the
> noblest among you in the sight of God is the most godfearing of
> you. God is all knowing, all aware. (Q49:14)

> For every one of you, we have appointed a path and a way. If
> God had willed, he would have made you one community so that
> he may try you in what he has given you. So compete with one
> another in good works. (Q5:48)

In defending an inherent pluralism of thought within Islam,
Sachedina writes:

> Religious pluralism for the shari'a was not simply a matter
> of accommodating competing claims to religious truth in the
> private domain of individual faith. It was and remains inherently
> a matter of public policy in which a Muslim government must
> protect and acknowledge the divinely ordained right of each
> person to determine his or her spiritual destiny without coercion.
> The recognition of freedom of conscience in matters of faith is
> the cornerstone of the Koranic notion of religious pluralism, both
> interreligious and intrareligious.[4]

Yet Sachedina quickly acknowledges that this Qur'anic spirit
of religious pluralism has been sidestepped by Muslims who
simply wanted political control over other people. When I
still hear some of the rhetoric from educated and seemingly
liberal Muslims living in the West, there is still this desire
to return to a period when the Muslim world was politically
victorious and the broker of all human relations. These are
imaginings which continue to ignore the complex social
realities of what is happening both locally and globally.

A large portion of the current discourse on Islam in the
world is really about political Islam, Islamism in the world

as opposed to Islam as a normative faith. The two are quite distinct debates. What does bind them, however, is the simple repetition of the phrase 'Islam is a complete way of life', which for the Islamists means that Islam must be the point of reference as religion, world and political order. Without generalising or simplifying too much, many Islamists and also many ordinary Muslims wish to reinstate a *khilafah* system whereby the global community of Muslims have a central figurehead, a person who lies at the centre of the Muslim political world as a reference point, basically a situation which sees the state playing God. Muslims often imagine a 'true' Muslim state where the 'real' Islam can be practised but most often have no real or concrete idea of what that means in practice, beyond simplistic formulations of ritual and piety.

One of the effects of globalisation in most Muslim societies has been the erosion of traditional methods of knowledge production and dissemination. Mass communication and literacy have led to diverse ways of democratising knowledge even though the decentrality of knowledge has always been part of the Islamic world. Now discussion forums involve imams, muftis and various lay and trained scholars who all become part of the public voice of Islam. Where does religious authority lie if not exclusively in charismatic, personified religious authorities? Who speaks for Islam in matters of politics, ethics, and so on, and what does it mean to speak for Islam?

As someone who has been engaged with the media, primarily broadcasting media, for most of her working life, I have always argued that I am not speaking for Islam but only commenting on an issue as a Muslim. When it comes to any issue that is 'overtly religious', the media, by its very nature, tries to encapsulate often in short pithy sentences whole areas of theological and ethical thinking. The result is that very often the political, religious and ethical complexity of any situation is somewhat lost and yet the media's huge reach dramatically influences the way people then understand a faith. In a globalised and technologically connected world, what happens on the streets of London reverberates in the mountains of Yemen; what matters in the revolutionary squares of Cairo provokes the debate about nation and state in the West. Language travels thousands of miles in seconds, and words shift in meaning across nations and cultures. Thus globalisation has an immediate local impact in a multicultural society so that how we understand the world may be how we understand our neighbour.

However, the French political scientist Jocelyne Cesari argues that the treatment of religion in the age of globalisation is extremely reductive, with the primary focus apparently on the phenomenon of fundamentalism. She states in relation to Islam:

> Islam is often cited as the example par excellence of such religious fundamentalism: in terms of its conservative or reactionary interpretation of the Islamic religious message, or in extreme cases, its sectarian usage and recourse to violence. The Islamic quest for authenticity is thus said to signal the definitive decline of the western Enlightenment.[5]

Cesari states that in the past two decades two different globalised forms of Islam have attracted more and more followers in different parts of the world. The first is the theological and political movements that emphasise the concept of *ummah*, the brotherhood of believers, such as the Muslim Brotherhood, the Tablighi Jamaat and the Wahhabi doctrine where the rhetoric is focused on encouraging a more fundamentalist approach to returning to the Qur'an and the Prophetic hadiths. The second form of global Islam refers to diasporic communities which develop solidarity beyond the boundaries of nations and cultures in the form of 'transnational networks'. The mobile dynamics of 'electronic religiosity has meant that Islam has expanded in all kinds of ways from audio/video to satellites, shows and chat room; the monopoly of traditional religious authorities has therefore been broken to some extent'.[6] It is largely within these fast-moving complex structures that Muslims living in the West are still connected to traditional forms of learning about Islam and connected to some ethnic-specific practices of Islam. Yet they live within the more secularised societies of Europe and America where their faith has increasingly assumed a greater visibility and a more public dimension.

The issue of the significant visibility of Islam began in my opinion not with the arrival of the first generation of Muslims who sowed the seeds of multiculturalism, but largely with the distinct wearing of the headscarf (*hijab*) from the 1980s onwards, worn by women of all ages. I well remember how this practice became a cause for debate amongst our family friends as we resisted covering our heads with the *hijab*, as it came to be known then. I am not sure how modest dressing, which has been a particular feature of Muslim societies and understood in all kinds of ways, was reduced to the *hijab* irrespective of what else these women chose to wear. We had grown up seeing our mother always in a traditional sari which she also used to cover her hair for any worship. She had never asked us to wear the *hijab*, knowing that we knew how and when to cover. Although we were never required to wear the *hijab*, there was a recognition that this rising trend would force a different and more narrow kind of discourse about

Muslim societies where much of piety and modesty would be judged on clothing alone. For me, this narrowing of Islam's diversity was disturbing. Notwithstanding the individual piety of some Muslim women who seemed genuinely committed, it reflected a disingenuous way of maintaining a more insidious control over society. During one of only a handful of invitations from a Muslim organisation, I was asked to address the topic of gender and Islam. The topic of *hijab* came up and I spoke about the scholarly debates over female covering. The whole session provoked angry responses from some women who exclaimed, 'Why is she here? All she has done is confuse us.' I smiled and replied, 'If you are confused, then my job as an academic is done.' I was a little dismayed but not surprised at the unwillingness to debate, although many young men and women came up afterwards and said softly, 'Thank you; this is exactly the kind of discussion we need in our societies.'

Veiling in all its forms – whether the *hijab* or the face veil, the *niqab*, or the full outer garment, the *burqa* – has become the central feature when discussing Islam in the West, and gender segregation, whether portable or physical, is seen by many Muslims as the expression of an ideal Muslim life. It has also rather curiously become part of the human rights discourse in the UK under the section of the European Convention relating to religious belief. Like many stories about Islam, the issue received attention through exceptional cases, but these cases all pointed to a growing social phenomenon. One such was that of the then leader of the House of Commons, Jack Straw, who created a national furore in October 2006 when he suggested that Muslim women should take off their face veils as it was a sign of separation.[7] While he acknowledged that he did not wish to be 'prescriptive', and

that the immediate context of his concern were the Muslim
women constituents visiting his surgery, the issue caught and
retained the attention of the media for days. The increasing
visibility of the *hijab* and the *niqab* has been one of the most
potent signs of Muslim female identity in recent years, an
image vacillating between relatively apologetic tones of
religious rights and freedom of expression and the critique
of physical and intellectual oppression. It has become an
embattled area in the field of Islam and feminism, with both
academic discourse and popular voices presenting a spectrum
of views challenging Eurocentric liberalism and advocating
an indigenous feminism. Its revival has created controversy
for Muslims and non-Muslims. As Keddie observes,

> One group denies that Muslim women ... are any more
> oppressed than non-Muslim women or argue that in key
> respects they have been less oppressed. A second says that
> oppression is real but extrinsic to Islam; the Qur'an, they say,
> intended gender equality, but this was undermined by Arabian
> patriarchy and foreign importations. An opposing group blames
> Islam for being irrevocably gender inegalitarian. There are
> those who adopt intermediate positions, as well as those who
> tend to avoid these controversies by sticking to monographic
> or limited studies that do not confront such issues. Some
> scholars favour shifting emphasis away from Islam to economic
> and social forces.[8]

Whether it is a call to reform Islam within or in response to
an ever growing global liberalism, Muslim and non-Muslim
voices have argued for and against veiling and the right to self-
expression, and some commentators have reiterated Samuel
Huntington's ever popular 'clash of civilisations' theory. But
veiling, especially the full face veil, the *niqab*, conjures up
an image of everything that the West has struggled against,

and for many people all the concerns about human rights, religious expression and political identity converge on this one issue. Where once the veil expressed the mystery and exoticism of the East, it is now seen by many as foreign, threatening and quite simply a regressive step in the whole intellectual fight for women's rights and equality. Anver Emon writes that the covered Muslim woman represents a very different trope so that she is now seen as foreign, and her mystery and sensuality have disappeared: 'far from being an enticement, she is a threat'.[9]

The Moroccan anthropologist Fatema Mernissi has argued and thus echoed a popular view that neither veiling nor segregation are grounded in the Qur'an and that if Muslim societies want to conform to the Qur'anic spirit of equality and justice they must modernise their attitudes and laws to both women and minorities.[10] This debate acknowledges that many women are voluntarily choosing to wear the *niqab* but contests whether this expression of their Islamic faith is really about piety or identity politics. The argument made by many is that the *niqab* symbolises a barrier to open communication and the equal place of women in public life. Rather than convincing the onlooker that it is about a woman's right to practise her faith as she understand its, this covering has become a symbol of denying women their full humanity. Whether one agrees with those perspectives which argue for or against female veiling within religiosity or human rights, the debate has become one of the most politically charged expressions of religious otherness today. Clothing has also been at the centre of a more recent controversy when in September 2013 a British judge had to rule on whether a Muslim woman could keep her face veil when as she gave evidence in court.[11]

But what women wear – and especially what Muslim women wear today – may reveal more about the onlooker than the woman herself. In relation to how men in different cultures understand a woman's intelligence and beauty, Mernissi takes the iconic figure of Scheherazade from the classic *A Thousand and One Nights* in another one of her famous works, *Scheherazade Goes West*. Mernissi makes a witty point about patriarchal control when it comes to female clothing, where she critiques how Eastern and Western men differ in their imagination of a woman's beauty and the harem. In a conversation with her friend Jacques who is showing her the museums and art galleries of Paris and who insists that the women in his harem must be 'nude and silent', she replies:

> Muslim men seem to get a virile power from veiling women and harassing them in the streets if they aren't 'covered' properly, while Western men like yourself seem to derive a tremendous pleasure from unveiling them.[12]

The fallout from the veiling/*burqa* debate has seeped into the political and philosophical consciousness of the West where it has become a regular reminder of the different conceptualisations of gender but how different cultures may choose to express their freedom and humanity. This has been explored, albeit briefly, in Roger Scruton's interesting analysis of *eros* and *agape* in *The Face of God*. Scruton argues that it is through understanding the face that we see how the subjects make themselves known in the world of objects. He defends the Christian understanding of marriage as a sacrament, and thus its purpose is to incorporate *eros* into *agape*, to ensure that 'the face of the lover can still be turned to the world of others'. Scruton claims that where marriage is not regarded as a sacrament and simply as a contract between the groom and the parents of the bride, the face of the bride remains hidden. Thus 'marriage does nothing to lift the woman from the private to the public forms of love'. He then introduces the *burqa* into his analysis:

> That is the *deep* explanation of the burqa: it is a way of underlining the exclusion of women from the public sphere. They can appear there as a bundle of clothing, but never as a face: to be fully a person the woman must retreat into the private sphere, where *eros* rather than *agape* is sovereign.[13]

The visibility of religious symbols and religious piety in public life is part of a wider debate about the meaning of public and private in largely secular liberal democracies today. What is public and what is private when it comes to religious faith has been complicated by the fact that in the UK there is no legal definition of religion and thus it comes into focus predominantly through discussion of legal and human rights cases. In assessing the multiple and complex reflections of religion and religious values today, scholars of religion have to address the issue of secularism and secularisation. In his seminal work *The Secular City*, the Harvard professor Harvey Cox provides a distinction between secularism as an ideology and secularisation, which is a liberating worldview, 'a historical process almost certainly irreversible, in which society and culture are delivered from tutelage to religious control and closed metaphysical world views'.[14] Secularisation, like religion, is difficult to define because today the term is used rather loosely and ambiguously in both academic and lay debates. Nevertheless, it points to one key factor which is that, at least in most of the West, religion has lost its public hold. Religion may still have its connective and collective attraction binding people together, as Charles

Taylor states, but society is now one in which 'faith, even for the staunchest believer, is one possibility among others'.[15]

Today one could be forgiven for understanding the religious and the secular as a conversation or clash between two homogeneous terms. This is simply not true, but it has happened for various reasons and partly because of the frequent media attention given to contesting whether religion is a force for good or bad in the modern world. Here, religious faith, especially theistic faith, is often seen as something which directs us to an intolerant past of conflict and confessionalism, whereas secularism grounds us in individual freedom and orients us towards a hopeful future. The debate has a simple premise which is that a gradual secularisation of most of the Western world has been realised through a conscious and enlightened distance between church and state, especially after the bloody religious wars of early modern Europe, leading eventually to healthy, liberal democracies. Yet, as observers point out:

> One should not forget that the Western notion of the separation of church and state is not only relatively new, but also under intense scrutiny and debate today. This concept has artificially compartmentalized religion, doing violence to its nature and reinforcing a static, reified conception of religious traditions, rather than revealing their dynamic inner nature. According to this post-Enlightenment perspective, any religion whose doctrines do not conform with the relegation of spirituality to the private sphere appears to be retrogressive. Increasingly, however, this approach is no longer dominant.[16]

The crux of the debate is not about religion versus the secular and their mutual interdependence, but whether religious expression is undergoing the kind of revival which may threaten or destabilise the relatively calm, well-ordered public and pluralist spheres of most Western countries. For many Europeans, a tolerant secular space is itself under threat from a competitive rather than constructive form of religious discourse. Religion is too often discussed as local stories which create global narratives. In recent years there has been a tendency to equate the specific concerns of religious bodies and institutions with special pleading. These stories and events resonate in EU constitutional debates especially when it comes to Muslim migrants. The laws of the EU governing migration increasingly demand reassurances from all migrants, but especially from Muslim migrants, that they are committed to the liberal democratic policies of EU member states. In 2003, the Commission began to monitor the integration policies of member states through its *Synthesis Report on National Integration Policies*. One issue that was stressed within the mutual integration process between migrants and their member states was that the 'religious beliefs of immigrants, in so far as they may affect the freedom from religion of others or the evolution of societies in undesirable directions, are seen as a legitimate subject of state regulation'. Integration is seen as a process of adaptation by the immigrants but it also demands a basic respect for the values of the European Union.[17] Thus, both migration policy statements and legislation have encouraged migrants to embrace 'European values' even though integration has often been seen as a two-way principle between the individual and the state.

To this debate must be added Europe's soul searching about her own cultural and political future. Many in Europe see her past and her future as Christian, while many see her past as Christian but the future as secular, a Europe where the public space is neutral social space and where the Islamic presence in particular, but also other religious voices, are becoming increasingly problematic. The Bulgarian scholar Tzvetan Theophanov argues that notwithstanding differences, Western European societies are deeply secular societies, but societies that respect individual religious freedom. The privatisation of religion here is the character of a modern secular society. Thus:

> These societies have a much greater difficulty in recognising some legitimate role for religion in public life and in the organisation and mobilisation of collective group identities. Muslim organised collective identities and their public representations become a source of anxiety not only because of their religious otherness as a non-Christian and non-European religion but more importantly because their religiousness itself as the 'other' of European secularity.[18]

Religion of course had never disappeared from the public arenas of these societies or from the way people expressed their personal and collective identities. However, religion has returned in a different way, not in a simple return to traditional forms of religion. This return recognises that religion may not be as emotionally fulfilling as it once was for many living in autonomous, secularised societies but it is still emotionally necessary.

In my own experience of providing expert reports in a number of legal cases dealing with Muslim or 'cultural' issues, the biggest hurdle is the conflict of concepts – what one holds to be outdated cultural practice can be defended by another as fundamental to their faith. Worse still are those instances of brutality and oppression which are often reduced to or made synonymous with cultural or ethnic customs and which have only recently come to be regarded as crimes. Over 10 years ago I was asked to compile an expert report in a murder case. An elderly Muslim man had killed his daughter by stabbing her almost 20 times when he found her talking to her boyfriend in her bedroom. The defence had asked whether by invoking cultural norms of honour and the man's Muslim background, a case of mitigating circumstances could be made. I replied no, that murder was murder and that religious or cultural references that were seen to justify the father's actions were quite immoral: the girl had committed no crime under any law whereas the father had. Such killings, known commonly as honour crimes, are not the same as domestic violence or even child abuse carried out by parents. Honour killings are in the main perpetrated by brothers against sisters, male cousins against female cousins or fathers against their daughters. While domestic violence knows no cultural or religious boundaries, there is a here a conflict of moralities. Families use the word 'honour' to mean that something good has been damaged and needs restoring, whereas the word is often reduced to meaning little more than preserving a woman's virginity at any cost. A communal sense of collective rights instils fear and demands obedience from women; when conformity is contested, violence is perpetrated.[19] The silence that so many girls and women keep out of fear can easily be equated with cultural respect. But respect requires equality and commitment to justice between the sexes. I think that there is something about violence against women, however horrific, which still doesn't capture our imagination in the way it should. True, we have come a long way in the West in terms of raising awareness of domestic violence, criminalising certain practices and simply being more sensitive to equal rights and dignity for all. But we still live with daily abuses of all kinds. In many Islamic countries, the spectre of the worst excesses of religious teaching hovers above society all the time, a threatening force always ready to silence a dissenting voice. Cultures change when mindsets change. When we live in societies where liberal freedoms are a given, we can't use these very freedoms to further oppressive behaviour. Worse still, such behaviour is often presented as in line with shari'a.

It is not surprising then that non-Muslim lawyers are left slightly bewildered. The problem with starting any conversation on shari'a is exactly where do you start? Misleadingly but commonly translated as Islamic law, the term has become synonymous with penal law, stripped of its broader ethical dimensions and the fluidity of juristic reasoning. As contemporary Muslim scholars attempt to contextualise the debates on Islamic law and ethics, they are constantly battling against the bloody-mindedness of some Muslim states which refer to shari'a as God's law but apply it only as a tool for self-interest and political expediency. God's law must be simple to be implemented. Unfortunately this sentiment is also rife amongst many Muslims in the UK who feel that shari'a is a body of immutable laws and that as law it must be applied without due consideration of time, place and individual moral agency. But the argument is even more complex than that. Aspects of shari'a are already in place here and where some are accepted, even encouraged, others are condemned for disregarding individual human dignity. For example, shari'a-compliant financial packages, while regarded by many Muslims as little more than a wordplay on the term interest, are nevertheless on the increase and our own Prime Minister sees the lucrative fallout from such religious convictions as London steers towards becoming the financial epicentre for such ventures. Dietary prohibitions on alcohol and pork are also part of shari'a, and formal prayer times, attitudes towards sex and sexuality, child custody are all part of the debate about shari'a. The phrase 'What does shari'a say?' is probably one of the most popular but misleading questions because it shows how simplistically shari'a is both portrayed and understood.

In the area of personal law, most Muslims marry according to their religious law and register their marriage under the civil law of the land. For decades this private religious law has existed within the UK and there is nothing here which contradicts the law of the land: no principle is being violated. But where there exist abusive practices within Muslim cultures, how does English or Scots law differentiate between shari'a as valid practice from shari'a as illegal? If arranged marriages are premised on adult consent, forced marriages, which unfortunately occur within many minority communities including Islamic, ignore this premise and should be seen as nothing less than a crime against the state and the individual. Many in the legal profession are aware that Islamic divorce proceedings are carried out in the framework of both religious and civil law. However, they are also aware of the vulnerable position in which this leaves women, who can become victims caught between two legal systems. The concept of shari'a as a unified and independent form of defined legislation in the UK is neither workable nor desirable.

It is interesting to note here the recent article by Jonathan Burnside who has written about the paradox of the place of biblical law in Western civilisation. Burnside writes that despite the Bible's deep influence on Western civilisation, our assumptions are very hostile to its having any influence at all in the modern world:

> From a modern perspective, biblical law is a spent moral force. We do not see its value as 'law', and so the subject has hardly any traction in modern law schools. Nor is the picture any better in other disciplines. It seems irrelevant to the study of anthropology, economics, politics and psychology, as presently conceived. The sole exception is theology and religious studies. Yet, even here, few curricula focus on biblical law. Usually, it is submerged within more general studies of Judaism and the Hebrew Bible. It is largely ignored in courses on Christian ethics.[20]

Our focus is on the text rather than what the text is about, and this is coupled with our reductionist views of the nature of modern legal studies. The Bible is seen as a set of rules, even commands, which appear morally unattractive. Burnside explains that if we look at law as a set of rules, this 'overlooks the way in which law, at the deep-structural level, consists of an endless permutation of legal relations, whether of rights, powers, freedoms, duties, liabilities, immunities and so on. It is law that shapes the vocation of society for law makes possible all kinds of futures.'[21]

The problem is not in the existence of religious law but in the nebulous status of certain aspects of religious culture. If it is argued that principles of fairness and justice form the basis of shari'a, then those principles should translate into different cultural and legal contexts to give them meaning. While it is always reasonable to understand why people do what they do, to be mindful of cultural nuances, there is no rationale for developing a different form of law-making which caters to a small minority within a minority. In the UK, Muslims are fortunate to worship and live as they wish; there is a distinct freedom here which is to be valued and nurtured rather than dismissed as if of little significance. Until very recently the concept of citizenship was silently assumed within all minorities who were British, but now this status carries ideological and political concerns. Much time is spent on discussing what it means to be British as well as English, Scottish and Welsh. There may not be much consensus on these issues, but there is still an agreed sense that the public space cannot be monopolised by any one religion or used in any way to disadvantage the majority of citizens. Some Western European countries are far more vocal and active in this respect. As Blandine Chélini-Pont argues in relation to France, especially concerning the headscarf:

> The French method is to raise the sword when the display of a particular religion enters into conflict with the population and with that which serves as its identity, that is, the Republican ideology, which is strong, unifying and without religion. It is a method that is clearly assumed, which could appear particularly repulsive to the outside. But the challenge of the method is, for the Muslims of France, to become French Muslims. Therefore, in discussing the problems that the Muslims pose and resolving them one by one, the idea is to resolve them within the sense of a republican ideology, and not vice versa, the respect of a religious particularity. This is the opposite of the English method.[22]

What is acceptable clothing in Western terms assumed an interesting twist in the Gérin Report of 2010 when it was claimed that the French ban on the full face veil did not go against the freedom of dress because Western civilisation had no such things as 'clothes for the face'. The Gerin Report emphasised the French republican values of liberty, equality and fraternity and had as one of its central arguments that the face veil eliminates the possibility for individual expression, thus disabling its wearer from being an equal in society. On this point the members of the Commission were clear:

> The face veil denies all individuality and thus all dignity to the one who wears it, whether she does so voluntarily or not. But the equal dignity of all human beings is the philosophical, even anthropological, foundation of the principle of equality in our Republic.[23]

The discussions on veiling in Europe are now immersed in complex ideals of freedom, femininity and faith. They are also about the shared public space. The political philosopher Blandine Kriegel, who worked for President Chirac, said, 'We believe in *laïcité* because we have to place ourselves in the public space, by abstracting from our individual characteristics, from where we came, our roots. This is the idea of the social contract.' What she is implying is that citizens should be presumed to agree, in the social contract, to abide by general principles. Although people can come with different traditions and histories, the movement should be from pluralism to unity through consent. The public space should be neutral with respect to religion. Prime Minister Jean-Pierre Raffarin defended the ban on explicitly religious symbols in public spaces in his address to the French legislature but also added that France was the 'old land of Christianity' and showed his commitment to the inviolable principle of *laïcité*. In the case of France, he added that religion cannot be a political project and '[f]or the most recently arrived, I'm speaking here of Islam, secularism is a chance, the chance to be a religion of France.'[24]

But what is the nature of this social contract other than equality under the law? From an Islamic perspective, the Muslim may understand his faith to be a covenant with God which takes precedence over the contract he has with any state, but is seems to me that observing both is important for the individual and society. The Qur'an commands that oaths and contracts be observed with whoever they are made, urging in several verses, 'Fulfil the contracts which you make'. Does this not relate to nationals of a country who have applied for residence and are living under the laws of that country? Muslims living in Muslim countries are morally bound to observe the rules and be compliant with the laws of the state from which they receive protection – to do otherwise would be tantamount to treachery, which is abhorred in the classical texts. Cheating and treachery are equated in the same breath in many Islamic traditions, for legal and ethical reciprocity is recognised between citizen and the state. For many contemporary scholars, the question of obligation to the state is upheld by the concept of contractual obligation and this involves abiding by the laws of a country, including all legal obligations such as observing the law, paying taxes, and so on. State security demands a tacit recognition of this reciprocity and for many Muslim scholars this has become the dominant position on issues of citizenship and social obligations.

Here we come to a burgeoning issue: the question of religious freedom. There is no one global paradigm regarding the question of religious affiliation, conscience or belonging. Different cultures, religions and societies reflect varying trends and practices on the issue of religious freedom. By religious freedom, I mean the individual right to practise a religion in public and private and also an attitude of tolerance/respect towards individuals who wish to practise their religion. Not all cultures or religions see religious freedom or tolerance as a value in itself. However, there has been a shift in the way many in the West, irrespective of their individual views on religion, view the question of a person's right to practise their religion, change their religion or reject their religion of birth. This lies in the fact that religious affiliation has now become an option rather than a necessity. Religion has changed its place in individual existence: from being a destiny determined at birth it has become the subject of a deliberate choice. It is the openness of this choice and the freedom to make choices that has become a defining factor of modern life.

In the UK, as in many Western cultures, religious freedom is located in the larger framework of human freedoms; this again is shaped by the human rights discourse which is based on the idea that individuals possess rights simply by virtue of being human. While many argue that freedom of religion is a right intrinsic to the monotheistic faiths, the modern shape of human rights as a totality goes back to the Enlightenment, which placed the individual at centre stage and divorced knowledge from revelation. Secular rationalism rendered human reason sovereign, making liberty the primary value of human existence, but there lay a tension between knowledge and moral truth. As Katarina Dalacoura writes, 'If the Enlightenment undermined belief in God and led inevitably to God's death – severing natural law from its origins in divine law – how could the moral worth and the inalienable rights of the individual be defended?'[25] Dalacoura states that by opening the way to the death of God, the Enlightenment undermined the beliefs which gave sanctity to human existence.

However much the principles are contested, it is not just the concept of human rights but their universality which has gained momentum over the last few decades. The roots go back to landmark discourses such as the French Revolution of 1789 and the American Bill of Rights of 1791. However, legally speaking, most states today accede to the 1948 Universal Declaration of Human Rights (UDHR). This has been followed by European conventions, all of which contain articles on the right to freedom of religion, which some argue is the oldest human right recognised internationally. The word 'religion' in this context is often accompanied by the words 'thought' and 'conscience', reflecting the view that a person's right to believe or not believe remains a fundamental principle underpinning human moral progress. Furthermore, such articles and conventions do not permit any limitations on the freedom of thought and conscience or on the freedom to have or adopt a religion or a belief of one's choice. It is not just what is in the mind that is important: you must have the opportunity to put it into practice, the ability to profess any religion in private or in public. I would argue that in Western liberal democracies, there is no religious persecution because of the innate overlapping freedoms which make up these societies. But the public space has become a kind of battleground. The paradox is that you are free to practise or not practise a religion, you are free to change a religion or reject a religion, but you are not free to blur the boundaries of public and private spaces. You can believe and say whatever you want in private, but the public space demands a different kind of allegiance, and the rule of law which can rule for reasonable accommodation often makes no exemptions because individual conscience and freedom of religion often clash with the law of the state which needs to make choices about how to protect everyone. The state is concerned with the defence of the right and not just the good according to John Rawls's definition. Political concepts are based on plurality, diversity and mutual limitations. As Hannah Arendt writes:

> A citizen is by definition a citizen among citizens of a country among countries. His rights and duties must be defined and limited, not only by those of his fellow citizens, but also by the boundaries of a territory. Philosophy may conceive of the earth as the homeland of mankind and of one unwritten law, eternal and valid for all. Politics deals with men, nationals of many countries and heirs to many pasts; its laws are the positively established fences which hedge in, protect and limit the space in which freedom is not a concept, but a living political reality.[26]

We live increasingly in a world of diaspora religious communities in which all religions are everywhere, often governed by largely secular regimes. While religion may continue to be a disputed term for a various reasons, it is used primarily as a system of belief and practice that accepts a 'binding' relation to a transcendent being. Yet even this does not give us a single essence of religion, since the conceptions of divinity and human relations with divinity are conceived differently. Many people of faith interpret morality and religion to mean the same thing in their defence of religious freedom in the public space. This further complicates the discussion, as if the state has no commitment to maintaining individual or collective morality. Even if we concede that much of the contemporary debate about religion/morality is less about personal conscience and more about the place of religion in public life, the issue matters for both the minority and majority religions in any one state. In the UK there seem to be two distinct arguments which only converge when both feel aggrieved by the state. The first is that multiculturalism has enabled the legal protection of minority faiths such as Islam, Hinduism and Sikhism at the expense of Christianity, so that Christianity alone has no protection from ridicule in the arts, media and general public discourse. The second argument rather simplistically brings religious voices together as a collective voice of conscience against the state's deliberations and subsequent laws on a wide range of issues such as marriage or the rights of sexual minorities, for example, homosexuals.[27] Thus there is the issue of the legal standing of religious minorities as well as the issue of all religions and their legal status. The legal cases that reflect the tension between public morality and seemingly religious exceptionalism show that in respect of the UK, a nation's moral consciousness is far less grounded in religion and authority than it was only a generation ago. In such a situation, can the state protect religious freedom when there are different ways of defining religion, different ways of practising the same faith – can lived religion in all its manifestations really always be protected by the law? Those who claim that their relationship with God has priority over their relationship with the state may have a valid argument regarding how they conceptualise and live their faith as a personal and public matter. Yet this thinking has limited weight when it rubs against the liberal state's own commitment to providing equality under the law for all its citizens. Whatever kind of social and moral leverage religious individuals or organisations wish to exert, rarely do political circles in Western Europe take such organisations as representatives of comprehensive ideological movements. Religious organisations can provide comments on everyday issues of wider public interest, but they speak as moral authorities only and, like other interest groups, must compete for resources and legal privileges.[28]

The essential question for many Muslims of all cultures is how do they wish to engage in civil society as *citizens* living in the West rather than simply as minority groups? Will the human experience of living and working with different peoples and cultures be the necessary factor in determining how pluralism will develop? For Muslims and Islamic states, this is about replacing the division of the world into the world of Islam and the world of the unbeliever by a world for all. It is about understanding that if diversity in all manners is truly God's will and a blessing on earth, it must be accepted intellectually as well as emotionally in real terms; this kind of commitment to diversity must make theological and political space for other ways of living and being, whatever the differences. Dogma and prejudice prohibits empathy with human diversity at a local, national and global level. If some Muslims see themselves as the Other in the West, they also need to be proactive in calling for an egalitarianism for all and not a division which separates the Muslim from all others. Muslim otherness in the West should not be a problem. The question is whether there is the will to do this in the first place and, if not, what is the distinctiveness of Islam that many wish to maintain? In other words, if some Christian theologians are calling for a new kind of civic engagement by the church where the Christian voice tells a story that is different from the one presented by the state, what kind of story do Muslims want to tell and how do they wish to share the public space? Furthermore, how can Muslim communities hope to be truly accepted in their religious otherness if so many do not exhibit tolerance but only demand tolerance? Islam has witnessed a renaissance in the last century, but many parts of the Muslim world are fractious and divided. Without reformulating the principle of political and social coexistence as a theological imperative and as a modern civic duty, Muslims will only ever see themselves as the dominant or as the victims; the *ummah* must be the brotherhood of all people, not just the fraternity of Muslims. This demands action at every level of society so that we can be compassionate and constructive players who are willing to realise a civic consciousness that is not just reactionary but truly visionary.

But Islam, for all its current otherness, is not the only religion undergoing a massive shift. Harvey Cox talks of a fundamental change in the 'nature of religiousness'. He states that in an age of globalisation, religions are becoming less regional and less hierarchical, and religious people are looking more for ethical guidelines than complex doctrines. Here, also, women are assuming positions of scholarly authority and leadership:

> As these changes gain momentum, they invoke an almost point-for-point fundamentalist reaction. Some Shinto leaders retort by emphasizing the sacredness of Japan, while the Barata Janata party seeks to 'Hinduize' India. Radical Islamists dream of reestablishing a caliphate that encompasses all of Allah's land. Some Jews want to establish a 'Torah state,' a holy land governed by scriptural law. The religious Right in the United States insists that America is a Christian nation. Literalist bishops in Africa and their American allies threaten to split the world wide Anglican Communion over the ordination of gays and women. Indeed, a core conviction of all fundamentalist movements is that women must be kept in their place. All these, however, are in the true sense of the word 'reactionary' efforts. They are attempting to stem an inexorable movement of the human spirit whose hour has come.[29]

As we witness civil societies on the brink of being torn apart in many parts of the Muslim world such as Syria, it highlights the fact that European societies have long recognised religion's totalitarian aspects and thus have limited the extent of religious influence in law and politics. The emergence of a common civil space where the religious voice is not silenced but is one voice amongst many has helped define the social fabric of most Western European societies. Notwithstanding issues of cultural and political pluralism, Muslims are part of European history and now stand at a critical crossroad in terms of what part they will play in Europe's future.

I find that I have lived with two themes most of my life – first, the absolute splendour of living in a society which is free and which allows you to speak freely; and, second, the gift of having learnt with inspirational educators who care, who want to leave the world a slightly better place, a more thoughtful place, who have shown me that we can all leave behind not just memories but a legacy. Maybe this is what Ralph Waldo Emerson meant when he said, 'Do not go where the path may lead, go instead where there is no path and leave a trail.' This is not about an unhealthy individualism or pride, but the realisation that we need courage in our lives to be all that we can; courage also to know that we are relational beings and that relationships of all kinds matter, including those we have with our society. There is so much talk of citizenship nowadays, but in the end, good citizenship is about being proactive, being visionary and being able to give of yourself and your time. It is the kind of society where, as Habermas said, citizens should be willing to get involved on behalf of other citizens to promote common interests.[30] Liberal democracies don't require perfect equality, but thrive on people of different backgrounds and beliefs being able to live together, feel that for all their material as well as cultural differences, they have a stake in the moral and public life of a country. There seem to be no more meta narratives about how to lead the good life; indeed, the philosophical concern appears to be about how to derive meaning in a life where meaning itself is contested. The virtuous life is not easy, but nor should it be trapped within religious–secular or private–public debates. If people really believe that it is this life which is, as Gerard Manley Hopkins wrote, 'charged with the grandeur of God', then it is imperative that all of us think seriously about the distinct contribution of the religious life to the public square, where certain values might transform a society's thinking. I don't think that the huge efforts made over the last few decades to promote a rights-based culture will be reversed simply because some religious authorities have different ways of understanding equality and difference. Human rights are not easily won: they are a constant struggle. For some in the West, modernity has brought about a kind of cultural and moral relativism, and only a more fundamentalist religious approach to issues of gender equality, sexual morality and end of life concerns can reassert certainty. For others, the changes to our social and moral climate, stemming from a greater emphasis on the autonomy of the individual, are welcome because they are liberating for the whole of society. However, when rights mean little more than individualism or entrenched ideals about private morality, then we are in danger of becoming selfish societies where our common humanity and mutual responsibilities and loyalties are eclipsed by the desire for personal satisfaction alone. In this climate there is no higher loyalty outside of oneself, no greater cause than one's emotional, even intellectual, needs. Indeed, if religious faith is only a projection of the self, lived in constant tension in society, it is liable to be reduced to simplistic demands and differences. Thus, the question is how does one restore the quality of the transcendent to the lives of people who are looking for a meaning beyond what they have already found in this life?

I think that having a sense of the sacred is essential in giving meaning and depth to our lives: a world without the sacred would be a completely different world. For some philosophers and theologians, the transcendent is right here on this earth and in our daily life. In his appraisal of the modern humanistic culture of the West, Don Cupitt argues that the modern West is the legacy of Christianity. He writes in the preface to his book *The Meaning of the West* that 'This radical humanist world – the world of everyday life, the world of the novel – is simply Christianity itself realized, or objectified. God has, at last, fully become human and only human.' For Cupitt, Christ is 'all there is of God; and now that Jesus Christ is dead and gone he in turn remains and acts in the world only in and through the lives of his followers'.[31] Cupitt talks of trying to reconcile church Christianity and the modern world, but states:

I ask: Why *try* to save the Church? It has been historically obsolete for about two centuries. We should let it go, and instead learn to see in modern Western culture itself the human and Christian values that we will need to proclaim and defend in the future. As we do this, we develop a new 'secular Christian apologetics'. We discard the institutional side of Christianity, authoritarian and power-hungry, with its supernatural doctrines, and instead we follow out the historical development of Christian spirituality and ethics.[32]

Cupitt's argument that over the last few centuries Christianity
has been transforming into a secular humanism, and is now
emerging in its final 'Kingdom' form, will resonate with
some. But Christianity, in doctrine and practice, is both part
of and separate from the West. The West is also innovative,
self-reforming, self-critical and always offering new ideas
about human freedom away from religious authority or
structural hierarchies. What the West does, it does in the
social and political contexts of liberal democracies. It may be
that liberal democracies have lulled us into thinking that we
in the West are now living in the best of all possible worlds,
as such democracies have gained almost universal legitimacy.
Francis Fukuyama's thesis is that the liberal *idea* rather than
liberal practice has become universal. He argues that no
ideology is in a position to challenge liberal democracy and
that although Islam constitutes a coherent ideology with its
own code of morality and political rule, 'this religion has
virtually no appeal outside those areas that were culturally
Islamic to begin with'. Yet as Fukuyama contends, we may
want peaceful lives but as individuals we are mostly restless
and passionate beings, in search of causes. Our primordial
instincts for struggle, our restlessness, is captured in his bold
assertions:

> Supposing that the world has become 'filled up' so to speak,
> with liberal democracies, such that there exist no tyranny and
> oppression worthy of the name against which to struggle?
> Experience suggests that if men cannot struggle on behalf of
> a just cause because that just cause was victorious in an earlier
> generation, then they will struggle *against* that just cause. They
> will struggle for the sake of struggle. They will struggle, in other
> words, out of a certain boredom: for they cannot imagine living
> in a world without struggle. And if the greater part of the world

in which they live is characterized by peaceful and prosperous
liberal democracy, then they will struggle *against* that peace and
prosperity, and against democracy.[33]

It seems to me that over the past few decades we have
talked of religion only as a problem and we have talked of
multiculturalism only to mean the Muslim population.
There is some justification for this and it may not be
surprising considering many of the global stories. But the
other story for me as a Muslim is the conversations which
Muslims are not having. Notwithstanding the current fears
regarding terrorism and the power struggles in so many
Muslim countries, there is a hesitation about, even fear of,
diverse ways of thinking and living within Islamic societies.
There is also a propensity amongst many to undermine any
kind of intellectualism, any critical inquiry about beliefs,
traditions, institutions and Westernisation, and to regard
only certain cultural norms as the true expression of Islam.
These are not symptoms of a yearning or of nostalgia,
but rather of a malaise which has made Islam appear to be
a social and political problem in the eyes of many outside
and inside the faith. Several years ago, someone very senior
within the UK security services asked me, 'What would
you say to white middle-class British families who talk of
Muslims as a problem at their fancy dinner parties?' I'm not
sure what he expected me to say, but I replied that I couldn't
stop anyone from thinking and saying what they felt about
the Muslim presence, but as a British citizen I could try to
make my own positive contribution to society in some small
way. Integration is a difficult concept to define, despite the
word being used so frequently, but I do know that being
British shouldn't make you feel any less Muslim. The choice
between loyalty to the state and loyalty to religion is false

and dangerous, but extremism creates this division, thereby destroying the possibilities of constructive community, national and international relations.

Yet for all these political and sociological tensions, all of us who believe in God must adopt a certain approach, one that combines humility with courage and that is reflected in the ordinariness of our daily lives. This does not necessarily require religious institutions or contrived leadership of sorts; it simply means that as individuals we have to be constructive players in imagining new ways of speaking and acting in public life, where religious faith makes a distinct and positive contribution to all that is important and worth living for. There is no one way to live a good and purposeful life and there is no return to a pre-multicultural society. Multiculturalism has evolved, but it continues to create a hierarchy of 'them' and 'us'. It continues to create imaginary bonds and real boundaries, but here in the UK, the Muslim presence can change multiculturalism from being a failed experiment to a success story. The responsibility to think and act is real and urgent because in the end, when politicians and think tanks claim that multiculturalism has failed, they are really only referring to one minority and one failure – Muslims.

SIX

Faith in God

I began studying Islam as an academic discipline initially through my doctoral research in Islamic law and classical jurisprudence. That period of research opened up a whole new world for me. Yes, I was raised a Muslim and knew the practices of my faith, but the scholarly/legal domain took me into new areas of thinking about my faith and its various intellectual expressions. Many of these traditions had little bearing on the way I practised my faith, but the gradual awareness of the complex history of a religion and its people made me see that the Islam of twentieth-century Britain was a diminished Islam, much reduced in grandeur, generosity and humility from its various golden periods. It was a realisation which took me on a particular kind of journey in my faith and in the study of my faith. My initial post at Glasgow University's Divinity School in 1996 marked the first Islamic Studies lectureship in the school's history; I was the first woman, first non-white and first Muslim to work at the school. However, while I was just grateful to get a job, it gradually dawned on me that in the eyes of many this post represented more than just a lectureship. The media were interested and the Muslim communities in Glasgow, communities I knew little about, were intrigued but sceptical. After all, the mid-1990s was a time when covering and wearing the headscarf had become increasingly commonplace in the UK – and I didn't cover. But not only did I not cover – I made it clear that if people wanted to judge me on what I wore, that was their problem and not mine. I wasn't concerned about people's suspicions about my faith, my apparent secular approach, but I was concerned about the way Muslims chose to speak about belief and practice in Islam. Although I think people's perceptions have changed a little over the years, for many Muslims, a woman's religious faith is still intertwined with what she wears. As late as 2013, after I accepted an invitation to speak at Blackburn Cathedral about Christian–Muslim relations, the Muslim lady inviting me wrote,

> It is vital that people, both Muslims and non-Muslims, meet and hear you, not only as an Islamic scholar, but as a Muslim woman who is not defined by certain attire. Unfortunately, I have also been criticised for inviting people who are seen to be representing a 'different' school of thought, especially when it comes to women, and Muslim women at that. I have often said that we do not always have to agree on every subject with everyone, but unless we create dialogue we are hardly likely to create understanding.[1]

What I once found amusing, I now find quite sad.

My interest in classical jurisprudence introduced me to a world of piety but also intellectual humility. Over the years, I have combined the methodology of exploring jurisprudence with theological reflections on Islam. Maybe some of this has been brought about by my interaction with Christian theologians, as I have always worked in divinity schools. This interaction made me see that while Islamic Studies was a varied and quite a robust discipline in the West, very few Muslim scholars were engaged in theological explorations with a spirit of critical inquiry. Islamic Studies was flourishing in the disciplines of history, law, Qur'anic hermeneutics, philosophy, politics and gender studies, but theological reflection which emerged from the lived experiences of ordinary lives, from the cultural zeitgeist of different societies, was mostly absent. Both for Islam and Christianity, many of the challenges of the present are essentially about the challenges of what is loosely known as modernity. The impact of modernity has been different for most areas of the Muslim world, which felt its overwhelming influence mainly through colonialism as opposed to the Western world which embraced it through the processes of the Enlightenment. However, modernity should not be viewed as antithetical to traditional religion, but rather seen in all its guises as in some ways a stark challenge to traditional attitudes to religion and traditional religious systems. One of the central questions of contemporary times is how we arrive at a meaningful interface between the divine and the secular. We should not view these two terms in opposition to each other, as very often they traverse each other's boundaries, but they often bring different approaches to our most complex human concerns. Over the last 60 years or so, much of the world has witnessed a certain fragmentation of organised religion, a desire by many to search for spiritual solace outside of traditional religious convention. Yet, despite the formal removal of religious ritual from many areas of public and private life, despite the many political and ideological waves that came and went, the major religions of the world continue to provide meaning – not because they can provide all the answers to the emerging problems, but because their theologies essentially embody two very human needs: a sense of conviction and a sense of hope.

As someone who has always been engaged in public speaking, I am often asked about my views on gender equality and female autonomy in Islam. Frankly speaking, I find many of these questions a little tedious but I know that the image and perception of Muslim women continues to be a hugely contested and divisive issue. The issue of gender remains one of the most controversial in Islam, with equal number of critics and apologists. However, in 2013, the world came to see and hear Malala Yousafzai, an Afghan girl who in 2012 at the age of 14 was shot in the head by the Taliban for promoting education for girls. Malala recovered, and in 2013 she emerged as a global figure, a symbol of all that a nation could aspire to. Education may be the one thing which, though a universal right, still remains an individual struggle for many. In Western countries, education is a given: your primary schooling marks your first steps into society; your secondary schooling shapes your entry into adulthood; and higher education allows you the opportunities to explore how you might make your own mark in the world. Yet for many across the world, education, especially for girls, remains their biggest dream and their biggest challenge. When Islam is used to attack education by equating it with Westernisation, the battle of ideas become fatal. Education for women isn't seen as a tenet of the faith itself, the guarantor of human development, but is denied due to fear that it may liberate women to think for themselves. Yet the whole emphasis on education in Islam seems to me to be precisely about that – taking the risk to reflect on the world and think for yourself. There are no boundaries to this sacred duty. This is why the particular prophetic saying, 'The ink of the scholar is more sacred than the blood of the martyr', is so moving.

In popular piety, the Qur'an is often read through a different lens nowadays. The Qur'an and indeed the post-Qur'anic literature are viewed predominantly as books of answers rather than books for reflection – and the two approaches are not the same. Religious texts have limited scope in providing definitive answers and they have always been interpreted in cultural contexts and alongside other sociological concerns. In 2011, the Muslim women's consultancy, Inspire, held a conference in London looking at issues of gender and authority in Islam. The Muslim scholar Michael Mumisa said:

> Over the years, most Muslims have come to accept and agree that the *tafsir* [interpretation] of the Qur'an or *tafsir* literature does not necessarily 'disclose' God's 'originally' intended meaning in a given Qur'anic verse but that it merely reflects the societies in which such interpretations (*tafasir*) were produced. In other words, we learn more about the interpreters (*mufassirun*) and their world than we do about 'God's intention' or the 'original meaning' of any verse.[2]

Islam is not the only faith trying to interpret 'original meaning', but it is the only faith in the West which to some outsiders seems to have stagnated in seventh-century Arabia in its search for meaning. The desire to recapture a 'true Islam' begins and ends in this century. It was at this conference that I first met the American Egyptian scholar and lawyer Khaled Abou el Fadl, who was undoubtedly a big draw for many of the participants. He is a rare type of Western Muslim scholar: what I would call, to use Christian terminology, a real systematic theologian of Islam. Theological reflection which links classical doctrine, especially Islamic law, with modern discourse and gives new meaning and a new understanding to the faithful requires knowledge, a scholarly but accessible writing style, courage and most importantly hope. It is hope that keeps us continually looking forward. For society to flourish we all have to be conscious of acting with personal, moral accountability and the sense of justice which doesn't hinge on whether you are male or female. Professor Fadl stated:

> All of us, as we look at our past, our present, and our future, whether we examine issues of civilizations or nations or gender, we have a choice in narrative. This is a narrative in which we imagine each other, we invent each other, we construct and reconstruct each other, and most importantly, we invent, we imagine, and we construct ourselves. The moral choice is one in which you could see a constant competition between human beings in a harsh, unfeeling environment, or alternatively, you could see a very different possible narrative. This alternative is the narrative of continuity and the interconnectedness of human affairs.[3]

Towards the end of his lecture, Professor Fadl spoke movingly about a certain futility in study alone. He said that before we delve into all this study, there is something more basic. It is 'all in a moment of piety, in a moment of true guidance, in this transcendental moment in which all blurs before your eyes and you see that we are but one in the eyes of God'.

In the end, I think this is true: we are all waiting for that one moment of transcendence. It is then that we will finally see that what we really wanted in this life could never be had, the reason for our yearning. C. S. Lewis speaks of the imperative to want more than civilisation alone:

> Most people, if they had really learned to look into their hearts, would know what they do want, and want acutely, something that cannot be had in this world. There are all sorts of things in

this world that offer to give it to you, but they never quite keep
their promise. The longings which arise in us when we first fall in
love, or first think of some foreign country, or first take up some
subject that excites us, are longings which no marriage, no travel,
no learning can really satisfy ... there was something we grasped
at, in that first moment of longing, which just fades away in the
reality.[4]

Lewis is not being pessimistic or disheartening; rather, he is
reflecting an anxiety particular to human beings who, even in
their times of happiness, are never truly fulfilled.

I have come to realise that it is not possible to be human
and not think of God; even those who refute his existence
must think of him in some way. As Rilke says, 'When I
say God – it is a great conviction in me, not something I
have learnt. The whole of creation as it seems to me, says
this word, without deliberation, though often out of deep
thoughtfulness.'[5] I am at a point in my life where I believe that
God remains the deepest and the most difficult presence in
our lives, however we live out our faith. I cannot imagine my
life without thinking about God – not through any ritualistic
performance or worship event, but quite simply as a thought
and presence I carry inside me all the time. I am thinking and
doing, with God in mind. This has happened gradually over
the years and while I can't remember a time when I didn't
think about God, I didn't always think of him as I do now,
moment by moment, a being I turn to, a relationship which
is part of me. I have gradually realised that devotion and
worship is a mutual experience, captured in the first part of
the verse 'So remember me; I will remember you' (Q2:20).
There is something profoundly moving and hopeful in this
verse. In many ways the whole God–human relationship in
Islam can be encapsulated in these words. Ibn al-Jawziyya

writes that God wants our tongue to be forever moist with his remembrance:

> Remembrance is the basis of gratitude. No one can be grateful to God without invoking Him. Bayhaqi mentions that according to Zayd ibn Aslam, Moses said, 'O Lord, you have blessed me abundantly, so show me how I can thank you abundantly.' And God said, 'remember me abundantly. When you remember me abundantly, you thank me abundantly; and when you forget me, you do not believe in me.'[6]

Remembrance is an ambivalent concept, taking on different forms. Some Sufi views contended that there was no recollection worthy of God, and that silent patience in the face of affliction was more appropriate than personal prayers. Others stressed the concept of satisfaction (*ridd*), of trust (*tawakkul*) in God, which allows no room to have any wishes of one's own. Anne-Marie Schimmel refers to Attar, who when performing the morning prayer asked, '"O God, art Thou satisfied that I am satisfied with Thee?" Then a calling came: "O liar, if you be satisfied with Me you would not ask My satisfaction!"' But most Sufis encouraged people to pray because prayer brings us nearer to God. God himself has ordered prayer so that he can honour man by answering his prayer, 'Pray so that I may answer' (Q40:62). Schimmel speaks of another more 'dangerous' view commonly found in mystics whereby God does not answer the prayers of those whom he loves quickly, so that he can continue to hear their voice. Conversely, if God does not love a person, he fulfils that person's wishes so that he does not need to hear their voice. For some mystics, prayer and words are only for the beginners: the true lover of God, who has reached the perfect state, has no need for words.[7]

Such views are both disturbing and moving. I first heard these kind of sayings from my mother and remember feeling uncomfortable at the time because I couldn't conceive of God without prayer – and my prayers were either of gratitude or pleas. While there are various Sufi perspectives on how to turn to God, to love God for God alone, most of us never reach that pious station and our lives hang between fear and hope. But these views were brought home to me recently at a conference where several Muslim women spoke about the ways they saw God as a presence in their lives. Towards the end, one young woman stood up and spoke of all the blessings in her life: her husband, her health and her children. What began as words of gratitude to God soon turned to an emotional cry as she went on to lament that God must have forgotten her because he had been so good to her. He had given her so much that she had nothing left to ask for; he was not testing her with pain or suffering in this world and she feared what lay ahead of her in the next life. I was moved by her sincerity and devotion but felt uneasy about her fears of being forgotten by God.

Remembrance of God is most visible in its ritual form through the performance of the canonical prayers (*salat*). Routine prayer contains its own virtue. Scott Peck mentions the Muslim call to prayer in *The Road Less Travelled*, in his section on the meaning of supplication:

> The little bit of Islamic theology I have read seems to contain the word 'remember' with unusual frequency. I think it is no accident that the Muslims build towers in their towns and cry out to the faithful five times a day to remind them to pray – and by praying, to remember God. The ordinary Muslim does as a matter of daily routine what only highly contemplative Christian monks and nuns do.[8]

In his work on spatiality and ritual prayer, Simon O'Meara states that 'ritual prayer is a type of travel', and the turning towards the direction of prayer (*qibla*) is the turning to God, a utopian travel. Ritual prayer promotes virtue and wellbeing in this life and the next. He cites Walid Saleh, who stresses the importance of orientation in the Qur'an, what Saleh calls the 'theology of orientation':

> The Qur'an weaves a matrix of words around the concept of journeying, guidance, path, and destination. It speaks of finding one's way, of getting lost, of roaming the earth, of straight paths and crooked paths (Q7:86); it speaks of lurking near highways to ambush, it speaks of stampeding on a highway; it speaks of darkness lit by lightning through which one attempts to walk, only to halt again as the skies darken, thus recreating day and night in an instant, guidance and bewilderment in the flash of a moment, while the believers have their light guiding them on the way ... Indeed the vocabulary is so rich and so varied, the imagery so complex and adroit that one has to take this imagery as fundamental in the message of the Qur'an as to how it understands guidance, and hence salvation.[9]

Our turning to God in this physical way is an outward manifestation of an inner longing. We turn to God who is a God in waiting, a God who also hopes that human beings will seek him. At one level, the Qur'anic story is essentially a story of struggle but not alienation from a transcendent God. In the stories of the prophets, it is said that Adam's disobedience followed by his guilt sees him wanting to flee from paradise, so great is his shame. He is accompanied by Gabriel from whom he asks for one parting glance at paradise, but is stopped by God at the gates of paradise. Adam implores God to turn him to dust again and the divine response is, "'O Adam, how can I restore you to dust, when

I have known for all eternity that I would fill the earth and hell from your loins." And Adam was silent.'[10] The Qur'anic verse 'I am placing on the earth a vicegerent' (Q2:30) alludes to Adam's purpose, in that Adam was always created for the earth and never destined to stay in paradise. His transgression is not a repeated theme in the Qur'an, nor is he set up as the origin of all subsequent human wrongdoing because Adam is already forgiven for his 'slip'. Adam must now experience distance from God to understand what nearness was. It is through this distance that the problem of predestined acts and free acts becomes magnified. A prophetic hadith encapsulates this dilemma faced by Adam and all those who followed him:

> Moses said, 'My Lord, show me Adam who brought us and himself out of the Garden.' So God showed him Adam. Moses said, 'Are you our father, Adam?' He said that he was. Moses said, 'Are you the one into whom God blew his own spirit, whom he taught all the names, and before whom he commanded the angels to prostrate themselves, and they did so?' Adam replied that he was. Then Moses said, 'What made you bring us and yourself out of the Garden?' Adam replied, 'Who are you?' Moses told him. Adam said, 'Are you the prophet of the Children of Israel to whom God spoke from behind the veil and whom he appointed to be a messenger from among his creatures?' Moses replied that he was. Adam said, 'Did you not find that my slip was written in the Book of God before I was created?' Moses replied that it was. Then Adam said, 'Then why do you reproach me for something that God had decreed for me before my existence?'[11]

The problem of whether God acted arbitrarily or whether this was extreme divine calculation remains unresolved, but lies at the heart of the human condition. In the Qur'an, Adam is forgiven by God, but in his one act of disobedience, humankind becomes destined to a life of moral choices. So it seems to me that human struggle was meant to be part of the human condition from the very beginning. This is the primordial story which reveals the fundamental tension in our relationship to God – predestination and human free will. Does human free will limit God's omniscience? It could be argued that for the most part, Sunni theologians generally denied that humans have the freedom to act and that it is God who creates our actions. However, free will was understood as a necessary corollary for the power to choose good, and for some, reflected ultimately on a God who is good and thereby takes a risk in the creation of humanity. Yet while we may cherish this freedom, it comes with its own burden, the weight of human responsibility.

Adam is forgiven in the Qur'an because he asked for forgiveness; he turned to God despite his shame because in the end God is our only refuge. Muslim theologians who spoke of turning to God spoke mainly of loving God, where knowing oneself was a prelude to knowing God. Ghazali wrote that 'when one knows one's heart, one knows oneself (or: one's soul), and when one knows one's soul, one knows one's Lord'.

Ghazali became one of the few writers to give a systematic account of love between God and man. He describes the mystical states and stations towards God by concluding that the love of God is the highest in rank and the last stage in drawing towards God before repentance and patience. Love is not a means to God: love is the end station, for the acquisition of the love of God is the end.

But can most of us love God in any great depth? We can discipline our desires, we can increase our piety and devotion and we can carry the sense of God inside of us – and maybe

FAITH IN GOD   199

this is what is meant by loving God. For Ghazali, love and obedience were mutually reflective but the lives of the ascetics and the mystics of history seems so far removed from the noise and distraction of our own daily lives. God is everywhere, but so much of the time we are struggling to find him.

Thus, it seems to me that we should act in this life as if we can turn to God for anything, any time. My relationship with God is essentially a selfish one, because it is me who needs him and who sees him as waiting. This sentiment is captured in a popular prophetic hadith which reflects a God in waiting:

> I am as My servant expects Me to be. I am with him when he makes mention of Me. If he makes mention of Me to himself, I make mention of him to Myself; and if he makes mention of Me in an assembly, I make mention of him in an assembly better than it. And if he draws near to Me a hand's span, I draw near to him an arm's length; and if he draws near to me an arm's length, I draw near to him a fathom's length. And if he comes to Me walking, I go to him running. (Hadith Qudsi, Al-Bukhari)

God's haste to respond to human remembrance seals the relationship of the divine with the human. It is said that 'the gatherings where God is mentioned are the gatherings of angels'. But in God's eyes, no human need is selfish, for he waits for every cry that is for him alone. In Ghazali's *Love, Longing and Intimacy*, it is said that God whispered secretly to David:

> O David, if those who run from me knew how I wait for them, how much tenderness I have for them and how I long for them to leave off their sins, they would die out of sheer yearning for me. They would lop off their very limbs out of love for me! O David,

> if this is my desire for those who turn from me, how great must be my desire for those who accept me? O David, man needs me most when he thinks to dispense with me. I am compassionate when he intrigues against me, but when he returns to me he is the most exalted that he can possibly be.[12]

God's longing for us, human beings turning or returning to him, has an underlying desire to it, almost desperation. But this desperation cannot have the same meaning we human beings associate with that word. Our desperation is borne of weakness, fear or despair. We often feel that we are lost in life or that we don't know how to live in more meaningful ways. As Erich Fromm explains, despite so much potentially within our reach for the first time in history:

> Modern man feels uneasy and more and more bewildered. He works and strives, but he is dimly aware of futility with regard to his activities. While his power over matter grows, he feels powerless in his individual life and society. While creating new and better means of mastering nature, he has become enmeshed in a network of those means and has lost the vision of the end which alone gives them significance – man himself.[13]

I think that most of the time we go through life not really understanding what it means to have true faith in God, even though we are thinking of God, because we cannot conceive of absolute surrender. I think about some of my personal experiences which intensified my search for God, for a new way of keeping faith alive despite all the uncertainties I felt. I realise that if your experiences make you who you are in your life, it is prayer which makes God present. When my eldest son was about nine years old, he suffered an eye injury at his school. A boy of a similar age had thrown a ball across the playground which unfortunately lodged itself in my son's eye socket. The injury was more than just a black eye and had caused a retinal tear. I can still remember the physical nausea I felt as the doctor explained the operation procedure; I wanted to be sick, sitting on the chair in that stark white room. When the day of the operation arrived, I waited with my husband and all I could do was pray quietly to myself; I don't think I had ever needed God as much. I looked around at the other parents also waiting for their children to come out from various kinds of surgery. Some were reading a newspaper while others were drinking tea and chatting. I couldn't understand how they weren't praying; how could they just act so casual? My son had his operation and his eye recovered eventually. Those three days between his first examination and the operation had filled me with a dread I'd never experienced before, a fear of the unknown and a complete powerlessness. It was also then that I realised how vulnerable your children make you feel and that your happiness as parents is dependent almost entirely on their wellbeing. I experienced a strange mixture of emotions: a sense of doom combined with anger. I wanted to blame everyone for his accident, but I also felt I was being tested for not remembering God enough, for not showing enough gratitude for all the blessings in my own life. I knew this was not the right way to think of God but it seemed the only way for a while. I blamed the boy in the school; I blamed the school for not caring; I blamed everyone even though I knew that this was a bad accident. My son's eye recovered and he never let it affect his school years or his cheery optimistic attitude to life in general. But I became a far greater victim of this event. It was a kind of turning point in my life: I worried more and I prayed more as if to find a new relationship with God.

Many of the current conversations I have on Islam
and God are with my children. As they get older they are
finding their own ways to express devotion and doubt. I can
encourage them to pray, to read, but I cannot impose faith;
faith has to be voluntary and from within. It has to mean
something to them in the present and in the future. They
enjoy an independence in so much in life and they observe
less markedly through rituals. But I know that I want them
to grow in their faith and that if they stopped believing in
God it would make me sad for them.

The Qur'anic verses which stress that God knows the
secrets of our hearts gives me some comfort, especially as I
struggle with issues of forgiveness. As a young girl I listened
to my mother recounting the various family disagreements
among her relatives. There were the fallouts which broke
people's hearts and went on for years, but often there was
forgiveness and reconciliation which united families and put
an end to feelings of exile and bitterness. My own family
conflicts have left me feeling unhappy with myself, in that
I couldn't see a way through, manage to forgive and come
to a new understanding with those I know I love. Islamic
thought on forgiveness is closely associated with notions of
justice. It is better to forgive those who have wronged you
than seek retaliation, but seeking just relationships is also
an imperative. Yet through most of my life I've realised that
justice is an elusive concept. It isn't a state we arrive at; it
is an ideal. And in striving for that ideal, we have to work
through the messiness of human emotions – feelings of love,
anger, jealousy and betrayal – every day as best we can. A few
years ago I was sitting next to a priest at a conference dinner.
It is sometimes with complete strangers that we feel the most
comfortable, and before long I found myself telling him about

my struggle with forgiveness. He looked intently and without any judgement or reproach in his voice said, 'The fact that you are so troubled by this means that you will eventually find the peace and reconciliation you are looking for. Don't be too hard on yourself, because forgiveness is always a two way process.' His words were reassuring and made me think that so much of our lives are spent on wondering how God forgives when we should be more focused on how and why we humans fail to forgive.

The voice of conscience must speak more loudly and more distinctly within me. Yet despite our own failings, the Islamic tradition constantly reminds us that God's 'mercy outweighs his wrath'. If we don't have hope, we don't have belief. There is no end to God's mercy because there is no end to God's goodness:

> O son of Adam, so long as you call upon me and ask of me, I shall forgive you for what you have done, and I shall not mind. O son of Adam, were your sins to reach the clouds of the sky and were you then to ask forgiveness of me, I would forgive you. O son of Adam, were you to come to me with sins nearly as great as the earth and were you then to face me, ascribing no partner to me, I would bring you forgiveness nearly as great as it [i.e., the earth].[14]

In Ghazali's writings we find several traditions defining the importance of hope as a basis for human devotion and worship:

> It is related that there were two devotees equal in devotion. When they entered the garden, one of them was elevated to the highest degree over his companion. So he said, 'O Lord in what way did this man exceed me in devotion on the earth? Yet you have elevated him over me in the highest heaven.' So God says, 'Truly, while he was on this earth he was constantly asking for the

highest degrees, while you were asking for salvation from the fire. So I have given every creature his request.' And this is a pointer to the fact that worship which is on account of hope is the more meritorious because love dominates the person who hopes more than it does the one who fears.[15]

I have lived most of my life with trust in God. In my personal and professional relationships, I have tried to avoid letting feelings of hurt and anger shake my trust in human nature. I find that most people you meet in life are good and generous, willing to help, and a question asked with a smile is likely to receive a response with a smile. I try not to worry about daily banalities, the little frustrations of life which are more often than not blessings in disguise. An ordinary day is always a good day. My children's studies, music and sporting activities, our holidays and friends bring joy and meaning. In many ways I feel encouraged to speak about matters of social and ethical concern because faith inspires. It is not arrogance or an attitude of knowing more than others, but a sense that faith needs careful expression because fundamentally belief in God is about hope in life. When I lecture to the public, there is an audience who wants to listen, to be reminded of the diversity of religious devotion and what religious faith with all its doubts and uncertainties can still bring to our lives today in awakening our civic and moral consciousness. Yet I am acutely aware that for many, religious faith rings hollow and disenchantment permeates people's lives. As far back as the 1970s, Christopher Lasch spoke of our changing sensibilities and argued that in the 1960s 'radical politics filled empty lives, provided a sense of meaning and purpose'. But today he states:

The contemporary climate is therapeutic, not religious. People today hunger not for personal salvation, let alone for the restoration of an earlier golden age, but for the feeling, the momentary illusion, of personal wellbeing, health, and psychic security.[16]

Our ideas of wellbeing, of satisfaction with ourselves, change throughout our lives. Religious faith doesn't always provide assurances, but there is no substitute for faith in God. When people write to me with gratitude and appreciation for a lecture or a broadcast, it is very humbling to know that you might have made a difference to somebody's day, to somebody's thinking. And what is particularly touching is that even though I speak from another religious tradition, the language of God has touched them.

But most of my life is taken up with my family and my work, and my love for both allows me to occupy a small corner of the world which feels safe. But I still fear that my faith in God will be tested through some personal tragedy, and when that happens, my faith might weaken. The very thought of a weakened faith is frightening because it makes you feel almost desolate. I think back to my mother's faith after my father's illness: whatever she was feeling inside, she never wavered from her prayer and piety. In some ways she continued to go forward day by day, with good days and bad days. There was a journey to be made each day, a kind of moving forward with God rather than reaching any destination. Religious faith is about the willingness to search within yourself for the truth and to be vulnerable to doubt, sorrow and happiness in this quest. As Andre Gidé wrote, 'we cannot discover new seas unless we have the courage to lose sight of the shore'. The Prophet's words, 'Seek knowledge from the cradle to the grave', do not offer any guarantees of where we might end up, but faith is essentially a journey of the self and it is in this search, this yearning, that the best of life is to be found.

Notes

Chapter 1: Home: Past and Present

1 This quote has been attributed to Ralph Waldo Emerson and Henry David Thoreau and its origins has a rather complex history. Please see http://quoteinvestigator.com/2011/01/11/what-lies-within/ (accessed 7 July 2014).

2 Amin Maalouf, *In the Name of Identity, Violence and the Need to Belong*, translated from the French by Barbara Bray, New York: Arcade Publishing, 2000, 102.

3 Al-Ghazali, *On the Manners relating to Eating, Kitab adab al-akl, Book XI of The Revival of the Religious Sciences. Ihya'Ulum al-din*, translated with an introduction and notes by D. Johnson-Davies, Cambridge: Islamic Texts Society, 2012, 30.

4 William Mckane, *Al-Ghazali's Book of Fear and Hope*, Leiden: E.J. Brill, 1962, 22. I have made a couple of minor changes to this translation for ease of reading.

5 Ghazali, *On the Manners*, 19.

6 Franz Rosenthal, *Knowledge Triumphant, The Concept of Knowledge in Medieval Islam*, Leiden: Brill Classics, 2006, 2.

7 http://40hadithnawawi.com/index.php/the-hadiths/hadith-26 (accessed 7 July 2014).

8 http://hadithqudsi.sacredhadith.com/hadith-qudsi-18/ (accessed 7 July 2014).

Chapter 2: Marriage and Desire

1 Rainer Maria Rilke, *Letters to a Young Poet*, translated by Charlie Louth, London: Penguin Books, 2011, 42.

2 Mitch Albom, *Tuesday with Morrie*, London: Time Warner Paperbacks, 2003, 127.

3 William Irvine, *On Desire: Why We Want What We Want*, New York: Oxford University Press, 2006, 2.

4 Murtada Mutahari, *Islamic Sciences*, London: ICAS Press, 2002, 205.

5 Ibid.

6 Shahzad Bashir, 'Islamic Tradition and Celibacy', in Carl Olson (ed.), *Celibacy and Religious Traditions*, New York: Oxford University Press, 2008, 140.

7   *Sahih al-Bukhari, Kitab al-nikah*, Vol. 7, Jeddah: Maktaba Darrussalam, 1997, 19 (Arabic–English translation by Muhammad Muhsin Khan).

8   Ghazali, *Kitab Adab al-nikah* in *Ihya'ʿUlum al-din*, Vol. 2, Damascus: Alam al-Kutub, 1992, 25. Further references to this work in this chapter will be abbreviated to *Nikah*.

9   Ibid., 26.

10 Abu Talib al-Makki, *Qut al-qulub, Sustenance of the hearts*, 2 vols, Cairo: Mustafa al-Babi al-Halabi, 1961, 2:528.

11 *Sahih al-Bukhari, Kitab al-nikah*, 20.

12 Roger Scruton, *Sexual Desire*, reprint, New York: Continuum, 2006, 62–3.

13 Ibid., 67.

14 Ibid., 359.

15 Abdelwahab Bouhdiba, *Sexuality in Islam*, London: Saqi Books, 1998, 95.

16 Yossef Rapoport, *Marriage, Money and Divorce in Medieval Islamic Society*, Cambridge: Cambridge University Press, 2005, 4.

17 Theodore W. Adorno, *Minima Moralia*, Frankfurt: Suhrkamp Verlag, 1951. English translation London: Verso, 1974, 131.

18 Christopher Lasch, *The Culture of Narcissism*, New York: W.W. Norton and Company, Inc., 1979, 188.

19 Milan Kundera, *The Unbearable Lightness of Being*, translated by Michael Henry Heim, London: Faber and Faber, 1984, 289.

20 Orhan Pamuk, *Other Colours*, London: Faber and Faber, 2007, 34.

21 Lasch, *The Culture of Narcissism*, 11.

22 Scott Peck, *The Road Less Travelled and Beyond*, New York: Simon and Schuster Inc., 1997, 34–5.

23 Karen V. Kukil, *The Journals of Sylvia Plath, 1950–1962*, London: Faber and Faber, 2000, 31.

24 Rilke, *Letters to a Young Poet*, 23–4.

25 Zygmunt Bauman, *Liquid Love: On the Frailty of Human Bonds*, Cambridge: Polity Press, 2003, 7.

26 Bouhdiba, *Sexuality in Islam*, 200.

27 Ibid., 231.

28 Bauman, *Liquid Love*, 45–6.

29 Ibid., 46.

30 Lasch, *The Culture of Narcissism*, 191.

31 Broadly speaking, these refer to the headcovering and the full face covering respectively.

32 Abdessamd Dialmy, 'Sexuality and Islam', *European Journal of Contraception and Health Care* 15:3 (2010): 160–8.

Chapter 3: Death, Dignity and the Passage of Time

1   Leo Tolstoy, *A Confession and Other Religious Writings*, London: Penguin Books, 1987, 35.

2   Jane Smith and Yvonne Haddad, *The Islamic Understanding of Death and Resurrection*, Albany: State University of New York Press, 1981.

3   http://40hadithnawawi.com/index.php/the-hadiths/hadith-2   (accessed   17 July 2014).

4   Al-Ghazali, *The Remembrance of Death and the Afterlife, Kitab al-dhikr al-mawt wa-ma ba'dahu, Book XL of the Revival of the Religious Sciences, Ihya"Ulum al-din*, reprint, translated with an introduction and notes by T. J. Winter, Cambridge: Islamic Texts Society, 2012, 15.

5   Abu Hamid al Ghazali, *Letter to a Disciple: Ayyuha'l-Walad*, edited and notes by Tobias Mayer, London: Islamic Texts Society, 1998, 28.

6   C. S. Lewis, *The Problem of Pain*, London: Collins, 2012 (1940), 101–2.

7   C. S. Lewis, *Mere Christianity*, London: Collins, 2012 (1952), 145.

8   Maurice Wiles, *The Remaking of Christian Doctrine*, London: SCM Press, 1974, 61.

9   Hannah Arendt, *The Human Condition*, Chicago: University of Chicago Press, 1998 (1958), 74.

10   Thomas Michel, in an inspirational paper, 'Christian Reflections on a Qur'anic Approach to Ecology'. Online at http://groups.creighton.edu/sjdialogue/documents/articles/michel_ecology.htm (accessed 7 July 2014).

11   Ibn Qayyim al-Jawziyya, *The Invocation of God*, translated by Michael A. Fitzgerald and Moulay Y. Slitine, Cambridge: Islamic Texts Society, 2011, 4.

12   Ibid., 26.

13   William Mckane, *Al-Ghazali's Book of Fear and Hope*, Leiden: E.J. Brill, 1962, 6.

14   Ibid., 45.

15   Ibid., 17–18.

16   Scott Peck, *The Road Less Travelled and Beyond*, New York: Random House Group, 1999 (1997), 162–3.

17   Sigmund Freud, *Civilisation and its Discontents*, translated by David Mclintock, London: Imago Publishing Co., 2002 (1941), 24, 26–7.

18   I have taken this analysis of Bauman from Masa Higo, 'Surviving death – anxieties in liquid modern times: examining Zygmunt Bauman's cultural theory of death and dying', *Omega* 65:3 (2012): 221–38.

19   Arendt, *The Human Condition*, 318–19.

20   Muhammad ibn al-Kisa'i, *Stories of the Prophets*, translated by Wheeler M. Thackston Jr, Chicago: Great Books of the Islamic World, 1997, 25–6.

21   Paulo Coelho, *The Pilgrimage*, translated by Alan R. Clarke, London: HarperCollins Publishers, 1992, 146.

22   Blaise Pascal, *Pensees*, translated by W. F. Trotter, 1660, http://oregonstate.edu/instruct/phl302/texts/pascal/pensees-a.html (accessed 7 July 2014).

23   Muḥammad Iqbal, *The Reconstruction of Religious Thought in Islam*, Lahore: Ashraf Press, 1965, 85.

24   http://edition.cnn.com/2010/WORLD/europe/02/16/pope.church.child.abuse/index.html (accessed 7 July 2014).

25   Michael Sandel, *What Money Can't Buy: The Moral Limits of Markets*, London: Allen Lane, Penguin Books, 2012, 10–11.

26   Laurie Penny, 'To save a generation from despair, it's not enough to hassle them into low-paying jobs', *New Statesman*, 10–16 January 2014, 21.

27 Bertrand Russell, *The Autobiography of Bertrand Russell, Volume 1, 1872–1914*, London: Allen & Unwin, 1967.

28 Ruth Macklin, 'Dignity is a Useless Concept', *British Medical Journal* 327 (2003): 1419–20, and Timothy Caulfield and Audrey Chapman, 'Human Dignity as a Criterion for Science Policy', *PLOS Medicine* 2 (2005): 736–8 (available online at www. Plosmedicine).

29 Peck, *The Road*, 162.

30 Blaise Pascal, repr. *Encyclopedia Britannica*, Chicago (1952). *Pensées* 168 (1670), trans., London: J. M. Dent & Sons, 1931.

31 Al-Ghazali, *Letter to a Disciple, Ayyuha'l Walad*, introduction and notes by Tobias Mayer, Cambridge: Islamic Texts Society, 2005, 14.

32 Hadrat Abd al-Qadir al-Jilani, *The Secret of Secrets*, interpreted by Tosun Bayrak al-Jerrahi al-Halveti, Cambridge: Islamic Texts Society, 1992, 48.

33 Jorge Luis Borges, *Labyrinths*, London: Penguin Classics, 1964, 206.

34 Ibid., 144.

35 http://dailyhadith.adaptivesolutionsinc.com/hadith/Three-Lasting-Good-Deeds.htm (accessed 7 July 2014).

Chapter 4: Christians, Muslims and Dialogue

1   Nile Green, 'Emerging Approaches to the Sufi Traditions of South Asia', in Lloyd Ridgeon (ed.), *Sufism: Critical Concepts in Islamic Studies*, Vol. 2, Oxford: Routledge, 2008, 1.

2   John Moorhead, 'The Earliest Christian Theological Response to Islam', *Religion* (1981): 11, 265–74. In the next few pages I have provided a glimpse into some of the Christological debates between Christians and Muslims. These have been taken from my recent book focusing on Christian–Muslim theological encounters. I am grateful to Yale University Press for allowing me to reproduce some of the arguments referred to in this chapter. For more, see Mona Siddiqui, *Christians, Muslims and Jesus*, New Haven and London: Yale University Press, 2013.

3   Hasan Askari, 'The Real Presence of Jesus in Islam', in Gregory A. Barker (ed.), *Jesus in the World's Faiths*, New York: Orbis Books, 2005, 142.

4   Daniel J. Sahas, *John of Damascus on Islam, The Heresy of the Ishmaelites*, Leiden: E.J. Brill, 1972, 133.

5   Ibid., 75–82.

6   For a translation of Luther's works, I have used Adam S. Francisco, *Martin Luther and Islam: A Study in Sixteenth Century Polemics and Apologetics*, Leiden: E.J. Brill, 2007, 113–16.

7   Luther's *Verlegung* cited and translated by Francisco, *Martin Luther*, 115.

8   Samuel Zwemer, *The Disintegration of Islam*, London: Fleming H. Revell Company, 1916. The book is based on a series of lectures Zwemer gave at Princeton, the purpose of the lectures being 'distinctly missionary', 9–10.

9   Ibid., 10.

10 Ibid., 181–2.

11 Sidney Griffith, *The Bible in Arabic*, Princeton, NJ: Princeton University Press, 2013, 176.

12 David Thomas, *Christian Doctrines in Islamic Theology*, Leiden: E.J. Brill, 2008. Extract taken from 'Abu Bakr al-Baqillani', 169–71. Thomas provides a useful introduction to the intellectual period of the writers as well as a synopsis of their main arguments.

13 Mahmoud Ayoub, 'Towards an Islamic Christology', in Irfan A. Omar (ed.), *A Muslim View of Christianity*, Maryknoll, NY: Orbis Books, 2007, 152.

14 Oddbjorn Leirvik, *Images of Jesus Christ in Islam*, 2nd edition, London: Continuum, 2010, 2.

15 Binyamin Abrahamov, *Divine Love in Islamic Mysticism*, Abingdon: Routledge, 2003, 5.

16 C. S. Lewis, *Mere Christianity*, London: Collins, 2012 (1952), 216.

17 Brian Hebblethwaite, *The Incarnation: Collected Essays in Christology*, Cambridge: Cambridge University Press, 1987, 63.

18 S. Nomanul Haq, 'Islam and Ecology: Towards Retrieval and Reconstruction', in Richard C. Foltz, Frederick M. Denny and Azizan Baharuddin (eds), *Islam and Ecology*, Cambridge, MA: Harvard University Press, 2003, 129.

19 Ian Almond, 'Islam, Melancholy and Sad, Concrete Minarets: The Futility of Narratives in Orhan Pamuk's "The Black Book"', *New Literary History* 34:1 (2003): 75–90, 89.

20 Ibn al-'Arabi, *Fusus al-hikam (The Bezels of Wisdom)*, translated by R. W. J. Austin, New York: Paulist Press, 1980, 174–8. For a helpful overview of select Sufi writings on Jesus, see Oddbjørn Leirvik, *Images of Jesus Christ in Islam*, 2nd edition, London: Bloomsbury, 10, 83–106.

21 Afzal Iqbal, *The Life and Work of Rumi*, 4th edition, Lahore: Institute of Islamic Culture, 1978. The verses are from the section entitled 'The Message of the Mathnavi', 189–90.

22 Seyyed Hossen Nasr, 'Islam and the Encounter of Religions', in Muhammad Suheyl Umar (ed.), *The Religious Other*, Lahore: Iqbal Academy, 2008, 92.

23 Joseph Lumbard, 'Qur'anic Inclusivism in an Age of Globalisation', in Muhammad Suheyl Umar (ed.), *The Religious Other*, Lahore: Iqbal Academy, 2008, 152.

24 Ibid.,154.

25 William Chittick, 'Religious Diversity, A Myth of Origins, Ibn al'Arabi', in Muhammad Suheyl Umar (ed.), *The Religious Other*, Lahore: Iqbal Academy, 2008, 280.

26 An interesting analysis by Richard Cimino can be found in '"No God in Common": American Evangelical Discourse on Islam after 9/11', *Review of Religious Research* 47:2 (2005): 162–74.

27 During the final stages of this book, the world watched with horror when a militant group calling itself the Islamic State or ISIS gained control over northern parts of Syria and marched into Iraq, killing many and forcing people to convert to Islam or be killed. See http://www.ibtimes.co.uk/frontline-isis-meet-men-children-britons-core-islamic-state-1460888ee (accessed 1 September 2014).

28 For three years, I was an associate scholar on a *Religious Freedom Project* at Georgetown University's Berkley Centre for Religion, Peace and World Affairs.

29 http://www.nytimes.com/2013/12/24/opinion/pakistans-persecuted-christians. html (accessed 2 October 2014).
30 http://www.project-syndicate.org/commentary/jihad-or-murder (accessed 7 July 2014).
31 Sigmund Freud, *Civilisation and its Discontents*, London: Imago Publishing Co., 2002, 48–9.
32 Zygmunt Bauman, *Liquid Love*, Cambridge: Polity Press, 2003, 78–9.
33 Hannah Arendt, *Men in Dark Times*, London: Jonathan Cape, 1970, 24–5.

Chapter 5: Religion, Multiculturalism and the Public Space

1   http://www.nytimes.com/2005/11/18/world/europe/18iht-brixton.html (accessed 7 July 2014).
2   Amin Maalouf, *In the Name of Identity, Violence and the Need to Belong*, translated from the French by Barbara Bray, New York: Arcade Publishing, 2000, 26.
3   Mohammed Arkoun, 'Rethinking Islam Today', *Annals of the American Academy of Political and Social Science* 588, Islam: Enduring Myths and Changing Realities (July 2003): 18–39, 21–4.
4   Abdulaziz Sachedina, *The Islamic Roots of Democratic Pluralism*, New York: Oxford University Press, 2001, 25.
5   Jocelyne Cesari, 'Muslims in Western Europe after 9/11: local and global components of the integration process', in Gabriel Motzkin and Yochi Fischer (eds), *Religion and Democracy in Contemporary Europe*, London: Alliance Publishing Trust, 2008, 153.
6   Ibid., 159–60.
7   http://www.theguardian.com/world/2013/sep/12/judge-allows-muslim-woman-wear-niqab (accessed 7 July 2014).
8   Nikkie Keddie, 'Introduction: Deciphering Middle Eastern Women's History', in Nikkie Keddie and Beth Baron (eds), *Women in Middle Eastern History: Shifting Boundaries in Sex and Gender*, New Haven, CT: Yale University Press, 1991, 1–2.
9   Anver Emon, *Religious Pluralism and Islamic Law*, Oxford: Oxford University Press, 2012, 270.
10 See her arguments in Fatema Mernissi, *The Veil and the Male Elite*, translated by Mary Jo Lakeland, New York: Perseus Books, 1991.
11 http://www.dailymail.co.uk/news/article-2421893/Judge-Peter-Murphy-rules-Muslim-woman-REMOVE-face-veil-evidence.html (accessed 7 July 2014).
12 Fatema Mernissi, *Scheherazade Goes West*, New York: Washington Square Press, 2001, 106–7.
13 Roger Scruton, *The Face of God*, New York: Continuum, 2012, 104–5.
14 Harvey Cox, *The Secular City*, London: SCM Press, 1965, 20.
15 Charles Taylor, *A Secular Age*, Cambridge, MA: Belknap Press of Harvard University Press, 2007, 3.
16 Jocelyne Cesari, 'Muslim minorities in Europe: the silent revolution', in John Esposito and François Burgat (eds), *Modernizing Islam: Religion in the Public Sphere in the Middle*

East and in Europe, Rutgers University Press, 2003, 251–69. Accessed on 7 July 2014 via http://www.muslimsdebate.com/search_result.php.

17 Ronan McCrea, 'Limitations on Religion in a Liberal Democratic Polity: Christianity and Islam in the Public Order of the European Union', *LSE Law, Society and Economy Working Papers* 18 (2007) (can be downloaded from www.lse. ac.uk).

18 Tzvetan Theophanov, 'The Twin Embodiment of Secularism and Islam in Europe: Analysis of Current and Future Trends', *Arches Quarterly* 2:1 (2008): 14–19.

19 http://www.theguardian.com/uk/2011/dec/03/honour-crimes-uk-rising (accessed 7 July 2014).

20 Jonathan Burnside, 'The Spirit of Biblical Law', *Oxford Journal of Law and Religion* 1:1 (2012): 127–50, 127.

21 Ibid., 127–9.

22 Blandine Chélini-Pont, 'What Is the Relationship between Stereotyping and the Place of Religion in the Public Sphere?', in Jesper Svartik and Jakob Wirén (eds), *Religious Stereotyping and Interreligious Relations*, New York: Palgrave Macmillan, 2013, 79.

23 See Kirsten M. Yoder Wesselhoeft, 'Gendered Secularity: The Feminine Individual in the 2010 Gerin Report', *Journal of Muslim Minority Affairs* 31:3 (2001).

24 Elaine Sciolino, 'Debate begins in France on Religion in the Schools', *New York Times*, 4 February 2004.

25 Katarina Dalacoura, *Islam, Liberalism and Human Rights*, London: I.B.Tauris, 1998, 7.

26 Hannah Arendt, *Men in Dark Times*, London: Jonathan Cape, 1970, 81–2.

27 For example, the issue of same sex marriage, http://www.bbc.co.uk/news/uk-politics-20680924 (accessed 7 July 2014).

28 John G. Francis, 'The Evolving Regulatory Structure of European Church–State Relationships', *Journal of Church and State* 34:4 (1992): 803–4.

29 Harvey Cox, *The Future of Faith*, New York: HarperCollins, 2009, 223.

30 Jürgen Habermas and Joseph Ratzinger, *The Dialectics of Secularization*, translated by Brian McNeil, San Francisco: Ignatius Press, 2005, 30.

31 Don Cupitt, *The Meaning of the West*, London: SCM Press, 2008, 19.

32 Ibid., x.

33 Francis Fukuyama, *The End of History and the Last Man*, London: Hamish Hamilton, 1992, 330 and 45–6.

Chapter 6: Faith in God

1 Email from Anjum Anwar, Dialogue Development Officer at Blackburn Cathedral, to the author, 3 January 2014.

2 Michael Mumisa and Khaled Abou el Fadl speaking at the Inspire Conference, 'Speaking in God's Name: Re-examining gender in Islam', City Hall, London, June 2011.

3 Khaled Abou el Fadl speaking at the Inspire Conference.

4 C. S. Lewis, *Mere Christianity*, London: Collins, 2012, 135.

5   Rainer Maria Rilke, *Letters to a Young Poet*, London: Penguin Books, 2011, 71.

6   Ibn Qayyim al-Jawziyya, *The Invocation of God*, translated by Michael Fitzgerald and Moulay Slitine, Cambridge: Islamic Texts Society, 2000, 85.

7   See Anne-Marie Schimmel, 'Some Aspects of Mystical Prayer in Islam', *Die Welt des Islams* 2:2 (1952): 112–25.

8   M. Scott Peck, *The Road Less Travelled and Beyond*, London: Rider, 1999 edition, 277.

9   Simon O'Meara, 'The Space between Here and There: The Prophet's Night Journey as an Allegory of Islamic Ritual Prayer', *Middle-Eastern Literatures: incorporating Edebiyat* 15:3 (2012): 232–9. Citation from Walid A. Saleh, 'The Etymological Fallacy and Qur'anic Studies: Muhammad, Paradise, and Late Antiquity', in Angelika Neuwirth, Michael Marx and Nicolai Sinai (eds), *The Qur'ān in Context: Historical and Literary Investigations into the Qur'ānic Milieu*, Leiden: Brill, 2010, 666.

10 Abdallah al-Kisa'i, *Tales of the Prophets, Qisas al-anbiya*, translated by Wheeler M. Thackston Jr, Chicago: Great Books of the Islamic World, 1997, 44.

11 This hadith has been taken from S. Murata and W. Chittick, *The Vision of Islam*, London: I.B.Tauris, 1996, 141.

12 Al-Ghazali, *Love, Longing and Intimacy and Contentment, Book xxxvi of The Revival of the Religious Sciences*, translated by Eric Ormsby, Cambridge: Islamic Texts Society, 2011, 98.

13 Erich Fromm, *Man for Himself*, London: Routledge & Kegan Paul, 1949, 4.

14 Hadith 34 related by al-Tirmidhi, cited in Ezzeddin Ibrahim and Denys Johnson Davies (eds), *Forty Hadith Qudsi*, Cambridge: Islamic Texts Society, 1997, 126.

15 William McKane, *Al-Ghazali's Book of Fear and Hope*, Leiden: Brill, 1962, 21–2.

16 Christopher Lasch, *The Culture of Narcissism*, New York: W.W. Norton, 1991, 7.

Index